The Last
Marathon

A Journey into the World of the Paranormal

Other Books by **Ruzbeh N. Bharucha**
published by **FULL CIRCLE**

- The Fakir
- The Fakir – The Journey Continues...
- The Fakir – Thoughts and Prayers

The Last Marathon

A Journey into the World of the Paranormal

Ruzbeh N. Bharucha

FULL
CIRCLE

THE LAST MARATHON

First FULL CIRCLE Paperback Edition, 2012
First Reprint, 2012
Second Reprint, 2013
ISBN 978-81-7621-231-8

Published by arrangement with the author

 Published by **FULL CIRCLE** *PUBLISHING*
J-40, Jorbagh Lane, New Delhi-110003
Tel: +011-24620063, 24621011 • Fax: 24645795
E-mail: contact@fullcirclebooks.in • *website:* www.fullcirclebooks.in

Designing & Layout: *SCANSET*
J-40, Jorbagh Lane, New Delhi-110003

Printed at Nikhil Offset, Okhla Industrial Area, New Delhi-110020
PRINTED IN INDIA
12/13/01/03/20/SCANSET/NO/NO/NO/OP250/NP250

TO

SAI BABA OF SHIRDI

ALL THE PERFECT MASTERS

AND THE UNIVERSAL MOTHER

Sai Baba of Shirdi

Avtar Meher Baba

Guru Nanak

Ketu Paymaster

Cheherazade Kathok

In sacred memory of

Cheherazade Kathok and Ketu Paymaster

Who passed over on January 1st 1978 in the

Air India B 747 crash, shortly after

takeoff from Mumbai

Introduction

I find it hard to believe that since *The Last Marathon* was first published over a decade ago, there still is so much interest in the book that it has forced me to re-print it.

Since the book was first published, much change has taken place in every sphere of my life. In all, seven books of mine have been published and three documentaries dished out to an unsuspecting audience. Since *The Last Marathon* was first published and now, in its third edition, I have through default or some cosmic shaggy dog mix up, channelled a few thousand times and have seen such heartening change take place amongst those who seek SHIRDI SAI's guidance that it has made life worth living and planet earth still worth strolling through. Mankind, when left to its own device is the grunge of creation. Something the cosmic cat dragged in. But when mankind gives divinity a chance, something celestial takes place and I have been fortunate to have witnessed spiritual transformation amongst my 'spiritual family'.

As *The Last Marathon* was out of circulation, it has been photo copied and distributed amongst the curious and the initiated. It has taken on a life of its own and all I can do is help it reach lives it is meant to enrich. I no longer recognise myself in this book. There was a child in me who has long since thrown in the towel and my life has gone through various changes; some hard, some beautiful; altogether amazingly surreal. While reading the book, I have cringed at my so called sense of humour or the lack of it. But I have retained most of the editorial as requested by all those who have enjoyed the book and who wish to pass it forward.

Since the first edition, I have gone through heart break and loss and have been blessed with immense gain. Personal thanks to Saina, whose love has made me the centre of her existence. Thank you for loving me, unconditionally; loving the man, the medium, the hippie and my restless energy. My three children, eldest daughter Vahishta, my darling son Pashaan and my youngest baby angel Meher (who I really feel has come down to hold her dad and help him live life to the fullest); always know that your dad loves you all. I may be with you physically or in spirit, but always know that my prayers, love and energy are with you all three, enveloping you, protecting you always, my precious ones.

Don't allow the world to make you bitter. Don't allow people and so called loved ones to make you petty. Don't let your self-respect be gauged and measured in financial terms or personal gains. Don't ever judge people. Be happy. Be cool. Let the child within you and the madness (which your dad has passed on) always keep you young at heart. Always live life as though your Master is standing next to you, seeing you, observing you, nurturing you. Don't ever let Him down. Nobody but your MASTER matters. Everyone else can go boil their beautiful heads. Always know that our Masters, SAI and MEHER, love you and are with you all, you three heart-beats of mine, always.

And when you are older and have a family of your own, once in a while, remember your dad and mom, with a smile and a JAI BABA.

Preface

I have often asked myself the reason for writing this book. I am certain that it is neither to fascinate nor to educate. There are far more engaging and absorbing books being written on varied subjects, ranging from the ridiculous to the sublime. Books written by psychics and those familiar with paranormal phenomenon abound all over the world.

I have nothing new to offer. Yes, the lectures delivered by Guru Nanak as well as the answers communicated by Meher Baba are original, but the contents are age-old. I am in no position to enlighten anybody. I can safely confess (my family and acquaintances will positively agree) that if there is a person who requires immediate enlightening, it is this author. I certainly do not want to preach. Lord love a duck, half of the problem facing mankind is that the preachers outnumber the listeners.

Could it be, that I want people to believe that not only does God exist but also that there is life beyond the grave, the crematorium or the electric chair (or in case the reader is a Zoroastrian) beyond the vulture's belly?

If a person does not believe in God then one can do really little to convince such an individual of the soul's immortality and its ability to communicate with the spirit and inhabitants of other worlds. I have neither the time nor the inclination to persuade him.

I also do not have the aptitude to make believers of those who do not want to let go of their prejudices. As the Bible mentions, no one is as blind as the person who plainly refuses to see and thus, acknowledge facts.

Money cannot be the reason for such a venture. Most authors often realise somewhere between the twenty-third and sixty-seventh rejection slip that there is more money delivering the morning paper than in writing a book. There is money in a number of ventures but trying to survive by authoring books! Buddy you are fighting against badly placed odds.

It was after a lot of thought that I realised the obvious. I wanted to share my experiences of the occult and the supernatural with those who enjoyed walking the mystical terrain. It was a journey I had intended to take since childhood and at the age of 30 I finally jump-started my rather rusty subconscious motor.

So this is how it sort of began.

"Mr. Bharucha! So we see you again at last. I remember you made us work overtime for an estimate of a liquor book which you wanted us to print the very next month."

"Ahhh yes!"

"Of course you forgot to mention that the next month was not of the same year."

"Ahhh yes but..."

"Why are you here Mr. Bharucha?" He too was speaking slowly and like my wife through his teeth. Amazing how people react to me! The similarity in attitude rises above barriers of age, sex and religion, truly marvellous.

"I...uh...ah...have two novels. Will you go through them?"

"If the main character is similar to you then the novels must for sure be tragedies. Am I correct, Mr. Bharucha?"

"Ahhh yes...I mean no. They are about relationships..."

"How to break relationships or how to bring about an element of exasperation to existing ones? Written by you they sure must be enlightening."

"Ahhh..."

"We don't print fiction but leave them here and come back after two months...and yes, Bharucha when I say two months I mean two months and not two years. If you once again disappear on me I promise you I shall find you in whichever unfortunate home you exist and stuff your own novels through any opening in your body I think advisable."

"Ahhhhh yes..."

"Two months. Be here. Now disappear."

The threat had made its impact. Six months later I entered Mr. Verma's cabin. He looked up with a smile. His smile froze when he saw that it was I who was standing in front of him with a wider smile. A soft whine left his lips and he rolled his eyes. He motioned for me to sit down. He continued with his work and then after ten-odd minutes, looked up once again.

"I liked the books. It is extremely hard to believe that you have written them...anyway as I mentioned last time, we have stopped printing fiction but I can give you a few references. You can send the manuscripts to them. I will give you a letter of introduction."

"Thanks..."

He wrote two addresses and handed them to me which I promptly lost the next day itself. Then he looked at me and pondered hard. I could make out there was a struggle going on in his soul.

"Do you want to write for us?"

"Sure..."

"But on which topics?"

"Uh...ah...hum..."

"What about liquor? You have edited magazines on spirits."

Suddenly something began to clatter in my head. Not with the same force as the chap who went about in the buff screaming his head off, but similar.

"Can I write about spirits?"

"Sure. Cover everything. From whisky to champagne..."

He rambled on. Meanwhile, I lit a cigarette and offered him the packet. We seemed to be on different tracks.

"Mr. Verma, I meant Spirits. You know life after death and all that jazz."

He looked at me as though I had gone mad and I inhaled a little too deeply. It took a few minutes for my nose to return to its original colour.

"Paranormal?" he inquired.

"Yes, yes I am back to normal. The smoke just..."

He banged the table hard. His face seemed to be changing colour too.

"I meant paranormal. Which means supernormal; metaphysical. Paranormal means beyond the normal. Not to be confused with abnormal; something you should be familiar with."

"Ahhh yes!"

He lectured me on how I should be living in the present and not in the clouds. He warned me that if I went about life irritating people, one fine day a sensible man would shoot me in the head seven times. Then he breathed deep, lit a fag, inhaled, exhaled and for some odd reason began to count softly, reached the number 10 and then once again looked at me.

"I will not be able to pay you much though."

I was well aware of this universal publishing phenomenon. We spoke for a few more minutes; then I stood up to leave.

"Bharucha, will I see the manuscript in a few years at least?"

"Ahhh yes..."

"Good. Now disappear."

I stood next to the gate of the publishing house and wondered about this whole paranormal stuff. I instinctively believed in life after death: angels, spirit communication, levitation et al. I felt familiar with all this psychic jazz and did not easily get surprised with miracles. I mean God is the master showman. He can do anything and everything in the blink of an eye. Of course, often mistakes do take place. Politicians, bureaucrats, publishers, marketing executives are good examples, but all said and done, God is the boss and I have no doubts about this fact.

But I did not know much about paranormal phenomena. Maybe I knew as much as the common man but how much does the common man really know about anything except how to combat the daily accelerating prices? We poor sods are so neck-deep in combating prices that there is really no time to seek higher intellectual pastures. So darn bogged down trying to live a few levels above the ubiquitous line of poverty that knowledge ranges from the 8.15 fast Church Gate local to the precise moment when the monthly pay is grudgingly handed over.

Standing on the road that sunny afternoon I realised two important things. I had somehow managed to agree to write a book on a subject which I had no idea whatsoever about and I had once again misplaced my mobike keys. I rushed into the publishing house and came out five minutes later with Mr. Verma behind me, frothing at the sides of his mouth but without the keys. I galloped towards the bike realising that for the nth time I had left the keys in the ignition socket. I saw the keys dangling and heaved a sigh of relief. I once again decided to at least begin a plan to get my life and general mental framework organised. I mulled over the usual observation from family and friends that I went about life like a bull in a china shop. Strolling about with head in the clouds and feet firmly placed on somebody's toes.

I returned home and placed the manuscripts under my wife's law books. The number of trees wasted to create one single law volume must be looked into immediately by environmentalists. I mean they weigh a damn ton (the law books not the green world folks) and nobody including the judges goes through the stuff. They are bulky and heavy and it is little wonder that advocates charge such phenomenal fees from their clients. It is the fees of lugging the dash books around. I was certain that these law volumes would not be touched for a few years and thus my manuscripts could repose in peace.

After the kids had exhausted themselves and the rest of the family, they slept the sleep of angels. I lit a cigarette and once again wondered why on earth I had got myself involved in the world of spirits and life after death. How did such a subject strike me? Why do I always get involved with weird things in life? Then I remembered my maternal grandmother with whom I had spent my childhood; a small doll-like woman, four feet 11 inches short. Aptly, her name is Dolly too. I have slept on her lap as an infant and cuddled in her arms as a child. I have heard her talk about spirits, sages and life after death when I was a kid. Yes, it was through her that I heard about spirit communication. I dialled the number.

"Hello..."

"Ma it's me." I spoke in Gujarati.

"Bol Ruzbeh, how are you son?"

"I am fine ma..."

"Did you get the job, son?"

Sometime back, I was the editor of a prestigious liquor magazine. Good pay, great job and then the bubble burst. I shall refrain from the ifs and buts and whys. Let us say God had better things in mind for me.

"Last week, I had gone for an interview. All went well. They really liked my work. They spoke to me for two hours. Promised to meet me for lunch and discuss the matter in more detail. Today I found out they have given the job to a person with no experience because the person is willing to work virtually free of cost and wag his tail every time the publisher calls..."

"Chhhchh. When are you going to settle down in life son? I worry for you..."

"Don't ma, the good Lord above shall provide..."

"Ha-ha!" That was my wife.

"Aren't you leaving a little too much on God's shoulders, son?"

"Yes ma, but what to do. It's either my shoulders or God's..."

"Then it is best to leave it on His shoulders. Anyway, tell me, why did you call so late?"

"Ma, do you remember you had once talked about communicating with the dead..."

"Yesss...."

"How true was it?"

"Have you grown so big that you can accuse your grandmother of lying?"

"No, no ma, I mean, uh...ahhhh...I mean do you still remember that incident?"

"Now you are accusing me of going senile and forgetting everything..."

"Ma! I'll see you tomorrow."

"Okay...uh...tomorrow means tomorrow, right Ruzbeh?"

I assured grandma and then lay down to sleep. Nobody seemed to take me seriously, I pondered.

"Ruzbeh..."

"Yeah..."

"Remember you said God shall provide." Such questions were tricky. Specially when the enquiry comes from one's wife.

"Yes."

"Then please tell God to leave some money in my purse. I have to buy uniforms and school books for the kids."

"Funny, funny..."

"And yes Ruzbeh, please tell God that I need the hard cash tomorrow. Good night."

I shut my eyes and pretended not to hear. These guys! My family!

Next afternoon I reached my grandma's place and announced that I was famished. We hugged each other and she piled my plate with her special dish: dhan-dar-patio. This is really steaming hot rice, preferably basmati rice, with yellow daal and a liberal spread of prawns in tomato gravy; less tomato and lots of healthy prawns. No one makes this dish like my grandmother. As usual, she sat down eating nothing but conversing and inquiring about me and my hyperactive family.

"I wish you had not lost that editing job Ruzu."

"What to do ma? It was either editing magazines on subjects I knew nothing about and thus making a mockery of my profession, but keeping the job, or handing over my papers and walking into the sunset..."

"Sometimes son, you must learn to compromise...but you were doing so well."

"That added fuel to fire. Maybe others did not like the fact that a gypsy like me could do so well..."

"For doing hardly any work at all..."

"Are you sympathising with me or what? I tell you sometimes I do not know who is on my side."

"Now what are you planning to do... I mean I doubt if I

will ever see you settle down in life, at least not in my lifetime. You are no more a kid, love. You are a father of two children. You are a family head...."

"Most people think I have a thick, fat head but great food ma. Now tell me about communicating with the dead." I smiled and winked at her. She sighed trying hard to suppress a smile.

"You know I was born in Iran in Nasrabad. My father's name was Nasarvanji and mother's Motibai Nasrabadi. I don't exactly know the year when I was born but I would say around 1915. I was the youngest of three children. I had a brother and a sister, your Homai Masi whom you know very well. When I was a month old, my father fell very ill and we all came to India, Bombay by steamer. None of us could speak any language but Persian, Dari. Actually my mother was born in India, in Pune, but she married and went to stay in Iran. My grandmother and my uncles lived in Pune and that is why we all came to India. But even in India my mother used to speak only Dari."

"My father died within two months of us coming to India and so my brother who was just 15 years old, had to travel back to Iran to take care of our family business. We had a lot of land and we used to export dry fruits to India. On the steamer, he fell very ill and died. May God bless his soul and may he rest in peace. They had to bury his body at sea. After losing her husband, the shock of losing her only son was too much to bear and my mother experienced severe depression which would often lead to a display of acute temper. I still remember her. She was very tall, far above six feet and beautiful and white as marble. But losing her son was too much for her and she was never the same again. Can you imagine, since the day she heard about the death of her son till the day my mother died 10 years later, she used to have only a loaf of hard bread with a cup of tea, once a day. She never ever ate a meal after my brother's death."

"Seeing my mother's deteriorating health, a number of my

mother's family members tried to convince her that my sister, your Mota masi, (elder aunt) and I, be kept with one of them. But for some reason my mother was against the idea of us living with either her mother or her brother's family. She knew that she would not live long but she was incapable of getting a grip on her grief. After a few years though, she sort of overcame the shock and her temper died down but still she never really recovered. Some years later she became a recluse."

"She permitted us to be adopted by a Parsee family, Faramroz and Temina Mody, who had just lost their daughter. Those days we lived in Thakurdwar's sanatorium. Ironically, I would live opposite the same sanatorium after 40-odd years. My stepmother and my stepfather lived not far away at Chikalwadi. So I used to meet my mother every day while my sister used to live with my mother."

"One day, when I was just three or four years old, we were visiting Jasmshedji Mody's glass bungalow in Bandra. I was playing with my sister in the garden when we saw a hunch-backed sadhu standing at the gate and watching us. He called out to me but my sister held me back and instead, she approached the sadhu. He asked her to give him a yellow flower that grew in the garden. My sister did as she was asked. In return for the flower the sadhu looked at my sister and told her that he saw a lot of suffering and hardship in her life. He was about to say more when a friend of Mr. Mody's saw this sadhu speaking to us. He felt apprehensive and approached the sadhu. This man was Dr.. Cawas."

"Dr.. Cawas rudely told the sadhu go away. He accused the sadhu's entire clan of being charlatans who lived by swindling innocent people. At this the sadhu got very angry. He shook with rage and said that in reality he was going to bless my sister but not any longer. He cursed the doctor that when the doctor would die, worms would crawl out of his body. A few years later when the doctor died, worms really did crawl out of his body and your aunt's entire life has been a struggle and hard work. Imagine she still works at the age of 83."

"Though my step-parents were really very good people I was heartbroken as my mother's health was getting worse. In those days, a very noble and powerful saint by the name of Arnat Baba would only raise his hands, give His blessings and then take leave. He never spoke a word. He was always accompanied by his wife. A lotus would be kept near her feet. Arnat Baba was from Hamnagar. He would give darshan in Bombay for a day. My stepmother, who saw me crying and worrying about my mother, took me to Arnat Baba."

"I still remember, I was crying a lot that day as my mother was not well. I had not wanted to leave my mother's bedside but my stepmother insisted that I visit the man of God. So I stood in the crowd next to my stepmother with tears streaming down my cheeks. All of a sudden Arnat Baba sent one of His devotees who took us to Him."

"He looked like an angel Himself and I stopped crying. He then took me on His lap and caressed my head. Then in a very soft voice He informed me that I should not cry for my mother. Now when I think about it, I wonder how He knew that the lady holding my hand was not my real mother. He then said my mother would live for a few more years and that she would never be bed-ridden. That she would die peacefully. He also promised that whenever I would be in trouble and I'd call out to Him, He would assist me no matter where He was. He blessed me thus and He has kept His word."

"Four years later Arnat Baba appeared in my dreams. He smiled and told me that He would no longer be coming to Bombay, not at least in his physical form. He informed that He was taking samadhi. A few days later my stepmother informed me that Arnat Baba had taken samadhi (when a sage consciously releases his soul from His body to unite with God)."

"Whenever I have been in difficulty I have shut my eyes and prayed to Arnat Baba and however bad the problem, He has solved it for me. You know that your aunt, Shiraz Masi had got burnt very badly when she was just a child. All the doctors had given up hope. They were certain that she would die. I shut my eyes and prayed to Arnat Baba. I reminded Him of His promise to me and within hours your aunt recovered. The doctors could not believe their eyes."

"Another God Incarnate I worship a lot is Sai Baba of Shirdi. I have been His follower ever since I can remember. Even now you know that I believe in Him a lot. But tell me why this sudden interest in all these subjects?"

"I am writing a book on spirit communication, life after death, psychics and God and His funny creation."

For a while she sat looking out of the window and then she sighed.

"You know what I find most funny?"

"Our politicians..."

"No. I find it funny that my grandson should be writing about psychics without knowing that his own grandmother and grandaunt have once been psychics too."

One adventurous prawn halted in its tracks, contemplated, decided that there was too much traffic in the food pipe and tried to detour through the wind pipe. I began to cough; then decided to lie on my back and roll up my feet. I thought it might solve the problem. But a few sips of water and three solid whacks on the back did the trick."

"You once were...a psychic?"

My granny smiled, stood up, took my plate and walked towards the basin. This was too much of a coincidence. How come I was not aware that my family had not one but two psychics? I mean this could not be a family secret! No family who has more than one woman can ever keep a secret for more than seven hours...unless the men are working overtime. Twelve hours at the most. And here I am already in my thirties, feeling 97 and still in the dark about the varied paranormal proficiencies of the women folk in my family. We sat in the drawing hall and I continued pestering my grandma.

"Why did you not tell me before?"

"I thought you all would not believe me so I kept quiet and anyway it is no big deal. Seeing spirits and being able to know a bit about future events is nothing great. So what? There are many who can do all this and more. You know, my adopted mother took me to Secunderabad when I was around seven or eight. My sister stayed with my mother and we used to meet every six months. When I was 10 years old I had a dream in which I saw my mother climb into a train. I saw her clutching her chest. I saw the doctors trying to save her. I saw her dying. And I saw her dead. I also saw my uncles and aunt taking her to the Tower OF Silence. I saw my aunts and sister bathing my mother and the Priests praying. Then I woke up crying. My stepparents thought I had fallen ill and rushed to my bedside. I told them that my mother was dead and they assumed I had had a nightmare. The next day we received a telegram that my mother had died. When I went to Bombay, my sister told me that our mother had died in the train due to a heart attack. When she described the entire scene to me, I had already seen it before. Even Arnat Baba had predicted that my mother would never be bedridden, she would die a few years later and while talking to people. That's how it happened!"

"I used to see spirits regularly but was neither frightened by them nor fascinated by them. All this paranormal business did not interest me and still does not. I married at the age of 12 and was a mother at the age of 14. My elder sister too can see spirits and look into the future. We had a well in our house at Secunderabad and every time my sister would come to visit us, she would make it a point to light a diva near the well. She could see the spirit that lived in the well and had repeatedly informed that it was a good spirit."

"When your uncle was around 19, a few nights before Diwali, I got a premonition that something bad was going to happen to him. A few days later my sister arrived and informed me that she too had a premonition that something bad was to going to happen to Noshir. Years before a fakir had told us that during Diwali when my son would be 18 or 19, he should not go near water or else we might lose him. We had forgotten about that incident as in those days we used to meet so many sages that it was difficult to keep track of all that they spoke and foretold. Now with both me and my sister getting the premonition, we made certain that Noshir did not go near the sea which was just across the road. But unfortunately we both allowed our instincts to be blocked by the prediction."

Oh yeah, of this calamity I was well informed. It goes something like this. Some ass who should have been swiftly and surely strangulated at birth put a powerful cracker in a rusted empty tin and lit the fuse. The edge of the rusted tin flew across the street and hit my uncle with such force that it cut the nerves of his leg, causing numbness. The tin had entered from one side of his calf and hung loose from the other. It was only when my uncle went home (hopefully after cuffing the moron below the ears and between the ears a number of times) that he realised the extent of the damage.

He was rushed to the hospital. The operation took place that very night. The next day all was well. Sometime during the day, some doctor, who should have been conveniently electrified and then parcelled off in numerous small packages all over Europe, insisted that my uncle begin to walk about in the large corridor of the hospital. (We are certain that the doctor's intentions were noble but sometimes when you work too hard, say six hours a day, most of the week, the grey cells begin to get wobbly. It happens to me at least.)

"So your uncle listened to the doctor and after some time blood began to shoot and spurt out of his leg. It flew all over the bed and on the wall. Fortunately my sister was working in the hospital. She had one look at my son and..."

My granny sighed and shook her head. "You know her, when something happens to a family member?"

I can visualise what must have taken place. First Mota Masi (grandaunt) must have yelled so loudly that patients about to die would have dreaded leaving their bodies, hesitant to further upset the Irani woman who was for some reason trying to break open the steel Godrej cupboard by using a doctor's head instead of the key.

"The doctor insisted on cutting your uncle's leg. They felt that it was the only way they could save my son as the poison had begun to spread through the body. You know your uncle was a very good cricketer. Maybe he would have played for our country. My sister felt that there was really no need to cut his leg. It was again a premonition. So we rushed to a psychic who used to contact the spirit of the dead. He used to charge Rs 500 per sitting. We contacted our mother who had passed away more than 20 years ago."

The medium used a planchette. A planchette is an instrument through which a medium communicates with the spirit world. It is usually a heart-shaped horizontal plank, either having an arrangement to fix a pen so that it can scribble on the paper beneath when it moves on the sheets at its base, or the entire board moves and halts at each alphabet when touched by a *medium*. So for the word "hello" to be communicated, the planchette moves first to the letter H and halts, then moves to the letter E and halts again, then it stops at the letter L, moves back a bit and returns once again to L and then moves to the letter O. Thus, letter by letter a message is communicated.

"Our mother wrote that on no account should Noshir's leg be cut. She said that he would be able to walk using both his legs but a problem would remain with his injured leg all his life. But his leg should not be cut."

The doctors were adamant that amputation was the only answer. But after a lot of convincing and a lot of brainstorming, the doctors decided to try and save my uncle's controversial leg. But they could give no guarantee for either the leg being saved, the leg being cured or for even the life of the patient. My grandmother signed the bond and my uncle still buys two shoes whenever he wants a new pair.

"But as our mother had told us, Noshir can no longer feel any pain in that leg. It has gone numb. Sometimes, even when a nail enters his leg he feels no pain. So he has to be very careful."

"Now tell me about how you can see spirits?"

"Nowadays I can no longer see spirits. I guess as one grows old, one's powers also deteriorate. But I can still feel them. Like in this house I know that the spirit of a man lives here. I get the smell of a Cheroot many times in the night..."

"But ma you mean this is God's gift"

She shrugged her shoulders. I knew that she was not even certain how to categorise as a gift, the paranormal ability to see spirits and be informed beforehand of impending calamities.

"When did you start seeing spirits...?"

"Who knows Ruzbeh. Maybe since birth, I don't remember."

"Does a spirit know you can see him or her?"

"I cannot see the spirit's face. I see the spirit in a cloudy manner but the face I cannot see..."

"What do spirits look like?"

"If it's a lady, I usually see her in white and a man too in white. There is a lovely fragrance about them. When I was young, I used to pray a lot. At least four to five hours a day. Those days I could see lots of spirits and lots of premonitions used to come to me. But then I never took them seriously and as I got more involved in family affairs, my prayer time went down to just a few seconds a day. Thus, slowly my power decreased. But still I can feel if the spirit is moving by. Any calamity about to happen, I see it in my dreams. I have seen the deaths of all my family members. Either as they really died or I saw them laid down in funeral clothes in the Tower of Silence. Now enough of all this, tell me, why don't you be like other people? More interested in money and living than in such silly psychic nonsense?"

I had never sat in a séance session (when a medium communicates with a spirit). I had never seen a planchette either. Of course, I had met a number of men who went into a trance. A trance-like state is achieved when a person allows his body to be possessed or occupied on most occasions by highly evolved spirits. Mediums go into a trance usually at a particular given time on a particular day. I have also met a number of mediums who did not go into a palpable trance but yet were spiritually guided by evolved spirits to aid mankind.

The first time I met such a person was just after concluding my SSC exams. My educational record was erratic. From the clouds I had found myself mingling with dust. When small, I was given a double promotion. It means the child is so intelligent that he or she can skip one entire standard or class and move to the next one above. From fourth to sixth directly, so on and so forth.

Anyway, I was given a double promotion. From the first standard directly I zoomed to the third. This was achieved either because I was slightly too clever for the teachers or may be it was a mutual decision taken by the entire staff to hasten my exit out of school, as fast as humanly possible. Till the sixth standard I was a "reasonable student". My teachers were reasonable while I was unfortunately their student. Till then my parents and family still nurtured hopes of me taking up one of the top-notch professions. Either become a doctor, an engineer, a chartered accountant...the good God alone knows from which spring of optimism parents nurture such crazy notions. If my children even complete their graduation, I shall go down on my knees and sing Glory Be to God.

After monitoring my academic performance upto the seventh grade, my father regretfully but confidently, threw in the towel. My mother, one of my greatest supporters, nevertheless assumed that I would fulfil their academic dreams for me!

"He will become a doctor..."

"And immediately be imprisoned for reducing the country's population drastically! I won't be surprised if one day he either becomes a journalist or a writer of books no one reads; or worse, he may even begin to write about spirits and ghosts. Trust me..."

But mothers are made of more resilient stuff. Either they have been endowed by God with more patience or just more foolhardiness. They do not throw in the towel so easily. They nurture the hope that their child, like the sun on a cloudy day, will burst forth and shine on the world. But even mothers have to sometime accept defeat, especially when their child's report card looks like the score card of the Indian cricket team during one of its slumps.

"Look at his card. It looks like modern art, all zeros and reds."

When I entered the ninth standard, a teacher who got along well with me, smiled and said with the right touch of professional guidance, "Bharucha, this year not even God can help you pass."

He was right, I flunked. My entire family seemed to be relieved. (When you are certain of a calamity, often you wish it takes place and you can get on with life.) Thus, when I gave my matriculation exam, I returned to Bombay (I studied in Billimoria High School in Panchgani, a small, beautiful hill station but what clinched the deal for my family was that Panchgani was far away from Bombay). My family wanted the best education for me...the farther from them the better. So as soon as I returned to Bombay, after a month, one day I was bundled into a taxi and my doll-like grandmother accompanied by a nervous father, went to meet a famed mystic and medium, Nawab Saheb.

My grandma had faith in him. Nawab Saheb sat in Poonam Chambers at Worli. I still remember the day. I even remember the thrill of travelling with my granny, who rarely left home as she worked 12 or more hours a day feeding us cousins and maintaining law and order in a busy house; and my father, who rarely came to Charni Road on a working day.

It was a fine sunny day. Not too warm and for me it was a thrill, travelling in a cab. Having spent my childhood in Panchgani, I was still half-witted enough to like cities. We passed Haji Ali and I bowed in obeisance at the dargha as well as at Goddess Mahalaxmi's temple.

We arrived at Poonam Chambers. Nawab Saheb used to sit there those days. A few people were seated in the drawing room. He would come out and solemnly invite the next person to join him in the prayer room. Time ticked by and after 20 minutes I found myself being welcomed by Nawab Saheb. He was a well-dressed, soft-spoken man. He embraced my granny, shook hands with my father and drummed my head. We sat down and each of us looked at the other to get the party started. My father softly inquired about Nawab Saheb's health and looked at me.

"Nawab Saheb, what will become of this boy?" My father was the last in line when tact and diplomacy were being dished out.

Nawab Saheb shut his eyes, then opened a three-inch small book, which now I recollect was the Holy Koran. He then looked at me and did what was becoming a common factor when dealing with me. He sighed apologetically.

"He is different...I mean, though he can do a lot he is very... uh...not lazy...very laid-back. Money and fame will mean little to him. He will do exactly what he wants to. He will nod his head and listen to you and then go and do exactly what he had planned earlier..."

"His mother wants him to become an IAS officer." Nawab Saheb smiled, my father smiled...both wanting to say: You know how mothers are, wanting an ass to memorise the Britannica Encyclopaedia. "I have tried to make her see sense but she wants him to become as IAS officer..."

"Only a mother would expect this boy to become an IAS officer. But the funny part is he has the capacity but not the inclination. Leave the boy alone. He will find his own water. He will take up an odd line..."

"Politician..."

"No, no. Who will elect him?"

"Ah that's true..."

"Nawab Saheb," fortunately for me, my grandmother entered the conversation which was becoming more of an anti-Ruzbeh tirade. "He has just given his exams; SSC, please see if he will pass and which class he will get..."

"Forget the class. Even if he passes it will be fine." Dad, of course.

Nawab Saheb nodded, asked me for my exam seat number, inquired as to when the exams concluded, then shut his eyes, prayed and after a while he once again picked up the Koran, opened the book and read a para. He then looked up, scribbled something and passed it to me.

"Seventy-one marks." I spoke nonchalantly. I was not surprised. I have sometimes got 45 marks out of five hundred.

"Seventy-one per cent." Nawab Saheb informed.

"Seventy-one per cent!" murmured my father and coughed. He was certain that my chances of getting so high a percentage were as remote as the probability of Marilyn Monroe walking in the nude at 2.30 in the afternoon at Bhendi Bazaar. My father knew it. I knew it. In fact, the whole of Panchgani knew this.

"Saheb, you mean 17 per cent," probed good old dad.

"Seventy-one per cent." Even Nawab Saheb seemed surprised by his own calculation.

I could see hope die out of my father's eyes. He had always placed Nawab Saheb on the upper rung of spiritualists. But now after this foolhardy prediction, Nawab Saheb was fighting tooth and nail to hold his place at the last rung of the spiritualist ladder.

In the cab none spoke. For a while we stopped by at Haji Ali and at the Mahalaxmi Temple. The sea beckoned.

"I have heard that if you get too involved with God and religion you go slightly out of the head. Poor Nawab Saheb, 71 per cent! Ha!"

A month-and-a-half later the results were announced. As I had expected, Nawab Saheb was wrong. I did not secure 71 per cent. I secured 71.2 per cent. Nawab Saheb was just .2 off the mark. This was the first time I had personally experienced the paranormal and I was for sure amazed and felt grateful to a benevolent Providence.

I have still not forgotten my utter amazement at getting so high a percentage in matriculation. But more than that, what I have never forgotten is the courage of Nawab Saheb to have faith in his prediction and stand by it.

My track record was well known to Nawab Saheb. He knew I had never seen the other side of 45 percent for years. My educational graph was at an all-time low. Any lower and forget failing, they would have had to demote me to a lower standard. He was aware of all this and yet he stuck to his prediction. He did not once double check what he had calculated. If he were asked to take a wild guess at what I should have got, he would have said 17 per cent, certainly not 71 per cent. It could not have been a guess. He could not have known from someplace else as the prediction took place long before the papers were even examined. This made me think. Generally as a rule, I leave the thinking for crucial matters.

But I knew that something extraordinary had taken place. Most important, I had passed and thanked a soft-spoken gentleman who was guided by one classy spirit.

Two years elapsed. All of a sudden, I became interested in Economics. I wanted to change my faculty from Commerce to Arts. I am not aware of what elders now think about the Arts faculty but in those days, nearly 15 years back, Arts was for the dangerous sex; only for the gals! Of course, that was also because not many were aware that in the Arts faculty, one was not taught how to paint like Van Gogh, but anything which was not accounts or science.

"Arts! What are you going to do after you graduate, draw? Ha!"

"But guys, this is not the art that you are thinking about. Over here they don't teach to draw..."

"Then why do they call it Arts?"

Such philosophical queries have a tendency of having me stumped.

"It is only a way of defining something different from commerce and science..."

"Tell this son of yours that his head will look different from others for sure, Arts!"

But economics had captured my heart. Just goes to show what asses we make of ourselves when growing up. Not even Arts, but economics! The family feud continued. On one side was logic, on the other my family, accompanied by lots of talk of violence, dark sheep, I -Knew-it-that-boy and ex-communication.

I was stunned. I mean, I was lusting after economics and my family made out as though I had impregnated half the damn college girls. The problem was that even my mother, grandmother, my eldest aunt, Nargish Bengali and my Aai, seemed keen that I should not take up Economics. They were the main propounders of the Pro-Ruzbeh-Let-The-Blighter-Live club. One day I was at Dadar. My parents and I had a major show down when suddenly a childhood friend of mine rang the doorbell. Then minutes later I was out of the war-zone.

"I am going to meet Bavaji. You want to come along?" I had heard of Bavaji. He was a Zoroastrian gentleman who had become an advanced man of God. He went into a trance and while in a trance a Mohammedan spirit would speak through him by possessing Bavaji's body. Bavaji used to go into a trance every Monday at sunset. He would remain in the trance till he had met all those who had queries or who wanted to be blessed.

At Bavaji's residence we had to wait in a queue outside the house. When we got into the house, there were only five people before us and to my surprise I recognised a friend of my parents. I was surprised to see him as he was a staunch Zoroastrian, who did not believe in any God men but Zarathustra and the doctrine preached in the Holy Zend Avesta. The line moved and this man stood in front of Bavaji. Bavaji was then a middle-aged man. Soft spoken, eyes open but far away. He stood with a cloth on his head and a handkerchief in his hand; behind him stood a few devotees who awaited instructions from Bavaji. Suddenly Bavaji looked at the family acquaintance and stared at him.

"So you have come here to test me." While in a trance Bavaji spoke in Urdu.

"I know you don't believe in me so why are you here? Why waste your time and mine? Go away! Never come back." He spoke loudly and in a voice that could melt steel.

I gulped. Why had I come here? Should I tell the noble man that I wanted to switch my faculty but my family, a band of commerce fanatics, was up in arms? Then I decided that if Bavaji and the spirit that possessed the former were God men, God-realised, then why did I need to speak out my problem? I felt my friend move ahead and touch Bavaji's feet to take his blessings.

"Don't be so stubborn. She is your mother and she has a right to scold you. You have no right to answer back." Bavaji blessed my friend, took the incense sticks, held them close to his mouth, prayed into them and handed them back to my friend. I gulped. Not even half-an-hour back there had been a civil war at my place, with me in the forefront. My mom and I had fought and I had spoken a number of things which I know I should not have mentioned. By God, I was going to get a mother of all dressing-downs, I concluded.

I bowed down in obeisance and touched Bavaji's feet for blessings. Bavaji put his hand on my head and for a while prayed. Then Bavaji patted me on my back and turned towards a lady standing behind him. Bavaji said something to her and she nodded and beckoned me to follow.

"Don't worry, all will go well. You are blessed."

I sighed with relief. At least I did not get a dressing-down. The elderly lady returned from the kitchen and handed me a plastic bag.

"Bavaji says not to worry. Take this lime and twice a day, rub it gently from your scalp to your toes, in a standing position near the place of worship. Touch it on your head and gently rub it on your body; right side and left side, seven times, twice a day. Take this taveez (amulet) and wear it around your neck; all will go well. Once your problem is solved throw the lime into the sea."

All the way to my grandmother's house, I pondered as to how I was to keep this lime and taveez without being spotted. If I was spotted then I was certain that along with the lime I too would be thrown into the sea. I realised that for a 17-year-old boy, life was getting far too complicated. Though my family visited God men, they were not keen to visit Babas who gave lime and taveez. For some reason they felt that this bordered on witchcraft and to make matters worse, to have a boy craving for economics and bringing home a blessed lime and a taveez! It was as good as a call for the declaration of war.

The first two days I managed to give the entire family the slip. Operation Lime used to be conducted while all slept in the afternoon and at night when they watched the video. Those days the video was a novelty, a new gizmo elders believed, was invented by the devil himself to lure children away from not only reality but God Himself. Operation Taveez was a simpler affair. I buttoned up my shirt to the top. The problem was that my family thought I was sick and would badger me to tell them how I felt and just to make them feel better I would say I felt ill; and it necessitated my taking medicines. Oh Economics, what hath I not done for you, you two-timing wench!

On the third day, disaster struck. While in the process of Operation Lime, I was caught in an embarrassing position, trying to touch the lime from head to toe. My grandmother yelled. I nearly swallowed the lime which at that precise moment was touching my lips.

"Throw the lime out now."

"I can't, it is blessed..."

"Why couldn't have God blessed you with some brains..."

"Ahhhh…yes, But I can't throw..."

"Either the lime goes out or you."

With such sympathetic, precise logic and multiple choices, I was at a loss for words. But I am a headstrong man. Once I decide to do something, I stick by my decision. Twenty minutes later, the lime and taveez floated in the Arabian Sea.

But what amazed me was that the next day all resistance to my taking up economics and joining the Arts faculty lost steam. It was as though all of a sudden the family decided to just leave me alone. One by one, the family members began a pro-Ruzbeh movement and within a week, I was given the green signal.

"I told you that day itself. If Bavaji has given you lime and taveez, your problem will be solved. He does not give these things to everybody, only when the person is in real need. That day, I think he must have given it to just three people out of 50," yelled my triumphant friend.

I waited for Monday to arrive. I bought two packets of sweetmeats; two packets for two reasons. One was that I had changed my faculty and the other, my eldest sister Kashmira had given birth to a son, Shiroy after many agonising years of ill-fated pregnancies. I met her, kissed the little one and off I went, to meet Bavaji. There was a short line that day, but it still spilled out of the door. I was standing outside the door, three people in front of me when an elderly lady came out and looked about.

"Has anybody just arrived from the hospital?"

"Ahhhh yes..."

"Somebody delivered a child..."

"Yes!"

"Then Bavaji says that come only after 40 days."

On my way back home, I sat in a daze in the bus. Nobody could have informed Bavaji that my sister had delivered a baby boy. My friend was not in Bombay. He was the only one of our acquaintances who visited Bavaji. It was impossible that somebody could have informed the good man.

In India, for 40-odd days, as long as the new mother menstruates, after delivery, a number of religious authorities advise family members not to visit religious places, holy tombs and dargahs. For many, it is best that when the new mother is certain that she is no longer menstruating, she officially washes her hair, a priest comes home, prays and then the green flag is waved, hence, the summons to keep me out.

I have met Bavaji a number of times. As recently as a few years back, with wife and two amazing kids. I realised recently that when in a trance, he speaks in Urdu but amazingly, after he comes out of the trance he does not remember a single thing he had said earlier.

Often, when somebody would seek clarification, he would stun them by inquiring what had transpired, what had been spoken and then, if possible, give an explanation. Often he would just shrug his shoulders and say: "He knows best", implying that the spirit that visited Bavaji knew best.

Once, the son of a close family friend of Bavaji presented the latter with his wedding invitation card. Bavaji held the card for some time, shut his eyes, opened them and looked at the young smiling lad and tore the card.

"Cancel the wedding." A stunned silence pervaded the room. The lad was obviously shocked.

"But...but...the wedding is going to take place next month."

"Cancel it."

If a man has been tested in conviction, then this was it. But so staunch was his faith in Bavaji that the wedding was called off. Obviously the girl's family did not take the cancellation silently. That too because some Bavaji, some fakir, had decided that the wedding should not take place. Anyway, the storm lasted for a while and life went on. A few months later the girl was diagnosed with cancer. She died shortly after.

During this time, my family was going through a private crisis. A relative, after a major confrontation with other family members, walked out of the house one rainy afternoon, promising never to return. From past experience, it was assumed that he would be back home latest by dinner time, demanding a hot meal. Well, they were wrong. When the next day he did not return, brows were raised in apprehension. Discreet inquires met with quizzical ignorance. When four days had elapsed, with no sign of the errant relative, the family activated the Bombay Police and contacted the hospitals.

All at home were understandably worried. Where could the blighter be? In the end, a number of psychics were requested to help but each gave exactly the opposite answers. If one said the relative was in Bombay, the next would suggest Timbaktoo. If one suggested the man was healthy, the other would sadly inform that the lad was fighting for his life. A number of them even mentioned the possibility of death. In the end, the inconsolable mother and her two daughters met Mr. N who went about his psychic business with minimum effort at conversation.

Mr. N listened, nodded his head and muttered that the relative was an ass and would be back soon.

Now 'soon' is a tricky, ambiguous word. A day could seem endless and sometimes a year seems to have passed in the blink of an eye. Two weeks elapsed. They once again met Mr. N, who shut his eyes and said that the relative was not in Bombay but some place near Bombay. He should be back sometime.

The word 'sometime' is a close relative of the word soon. Anyway, six months elapsed. At the last count, three psychics said the relative was dead, two divulged that he was lying unconscious and four informed that the good man was ensnared by a woman who would not part with him. In the end the mother decided to thrash things out once and for all. She had faith in Mr. N. He had never been wrong. Yes, sometimes he did go off track but it was rare. She met Mr. N.

"Why don't you tell me once and for all where he is? Is he alive or dead? Once and for all!"

Mr. N sighed and shut his eyes. He knew that if he tried to evade the question he could get a clip on the knuckles and a whack on the ear. The woman was at the end of her tether, she looked serious and on the verge of an explosion. Since childhood Mr. N had been taught that an angry mother, a hungry tiger and a volcano about to burst, should be religiously avoided.'

"The last day of the next month one of your daughters shall find your son."

"Sure."

"If not, don't come to me. I have told you all that I can predict."

Last day of the next month, the man's elder sister was returning home late in the evening. The over-bridge lamp was burning low. Visibility on the flyover was poor. The daughter tripped over somebody, sleeping in the darkness on the bridge.

She turned to apologise. The absconding relative smiled sheepishly. She had found her wayward brother. As prophesied, the relative had been found on the last day of the proposed month by his sister!

When I was in college, my paternal grandmother fell very ill. Even doctors voiced concern over her health and so my aunt took a photograph of her to Nawab Saheb. My paternal grandparents smiled back from the photograph. Nawab Saheb shut his eyes, prayed and then opened the Koran. He then read a para, shut his eyes and after a while looked at my aunt.

This lady will live for another five years but this gentleman; standing near her will die before the year's end. "

My aunt was naturally shocked. My grandfather was a healthy, robust man who, though in his eighties, still had strength to knock down a young over-zealous boxer. He was healthy as a stalwart horse and except for failing eyesight and a recent limp, time had marked him lightly.

"But he is in very good health," emphasised my aunt.

The seer shrugged his shoulders, smiled and stood up to indicate that the meeting was over. On December 25, 12.15 in the morning, when the world was celebrating the birth of Christ, my grandpa breathed his last. He was in good health till the very end. Though the seer's prediction was accurate, what surprised us was the fact that hours before he expired, my grandfather was aware that he would not live long. He was a very religious man. He prayed all through the day but still retained his joy for living. On the last day of his life, as soon as he woke up, he wished all a Merry Christmas and in advance, a Happy New Year. When inquired by family members why he was wishing all in advance, he replied that maybe he would not be present for the New Year, a premonition that his time had arrived!

I remember another instance of a premonition. There was a man who, though very powerful in astrology, did not accommodate those who wanted a glimpse of the future. But if in the mood, he would oblige by looking ahead in time. One morning as he woke up, he requested his wife, as per traditional Parsi custom, to hang a huge garland of flowers at the entrance of their Home and decorate the floor with designs made from lime and chalk. He asked her to prepare a celebratory breakfast of sev (vermicelli) and curd and for lunch, rice-dal-fish sauce; two dishes traditionally reserved for festive days. He then went for a bath, wore a new sudra, kusti, pyjama and had breakfast along with his wife and son. Both wife and son were slightly mystified with this behaviour. To add to the mystery, he asked his son to skip work that day. Then the family sat down and talked about old times. At lunch once again, they all sat and ate the traditional Parsi festive meal. After lunch, he sat with his family, spoke for some time and then stood up.

"Come wish me goodbye. You shall no longer see me alive once I enter the room."

They were shocked. Both assumed that maybe he had suddenly taken ill. They felt that he should rest. After a good sleep, this depressive feeling of lurking death would abate. But nonetheless, he embraced them warmly and entered the room. An hour later the wife entered the room to have a look at her husband. She found to her shock that her husband had been telling them the truth. He lay dead, a look of peace on his face.

Maybe all these experiences made me want to dwell more in the transcendental world. But the problem was that I did not know where to start. I knew no medium who communicated with the spirit world. I did not know anyone who knew such a medium. So I decided to inquire among my family and friends. They, as usual, were at their helpful best. A few of my family members laughed so loud that they did not hear me bang the door while going for a walk. Of course, a number of them were brimming with assistance.

"So you want to communicate with spirits, huh?"

"Ahhh…yes."

"Why don't you start communicating with mankind first? We leave messages everyday on your pager and still receive no response from you and now you want to communicate with spirits, huh? "

So I decided that I would speak to my wife and together, husband and wife…for better or for worse, good health and bad, cash or credit, till death do us apart – we would work on the project. Talk of illusions!

"If because of you, some stupid, inquisitive spirit begins to haunt me, Ruzbeh Bharucha, I shall divorce you that very moment…"

"In front of the spirit…"

"Don't try getting funny, please. My God! How could I have fallen in love with some crackpot like you? And tell me, why do you want to know whether spirits communicate? You men barely communicate when you all are alive…."

"Ahhhh yes."

Back to square one. I needed a medium. Now who is a medium? A medium is a person through whom communication is made between the living and those in the spirit world. I knew of a very famous medium but for some odd reason, odd then, a soft voice within me insisted that I avoid her.

"Why?" I inquired of the soft voice within me.

"Because I say so."

"That is not very democratic."

"Listen to me once and for all."

"Okay."

"Just shut up and avoid that lady."

"But if I go to her, my life will become so much easier."

I assumed that where my overpowering personality had failed to create an impression, my logic, sharp and precise, would get home the bacon. The voice within me was silent for a long time. My logic has this power over people. It just leaves them speechless.

"If you really want to make life easy for yourself and for those unfortunately associated with you, then stop pretending that you have a brain and that you think once in a random while. Just shut up and listen to me. Wants to make life easier! Ha!"

A month strolled by, not a dash medium in sight. I spoke with a sympathetic friend.

"Why don't you see that famous medium?"

"I can't."

"Why not?"

"It's a long story." Anyway, I spoke to him about soft-voice-losing-battle.

"It stops me."

"The only thing stopping you from seeing that woman is your pale green cells. Not grey cells mind you. They have turned pale green from misuse." He then held his belly and roared uproariously. I tell you these guys!

Then fortunately, my uncle returned to India after nearly two-and-a-half decades of working abroad. Mr. Dali Mohta is an extremely learned man in the field of spiritualism, who knows more about different religions, their customs and folklore and traditions, than anyone I have met. In his younger days he was involved with the same mystical business that I had unconsciously stumbled upon. Obviously, he did not have the soft tyrannical voices giving him orders and obdurately refusing to listen to good, healthy sense. One day we met and I told him of my predicament.

"Why don't you meet that famous medium?"

"I can't. Something is stopping me from seeing her."

I spoke, waiting to hear similar scoffing poetry. But amazingly he did not show either surprise or adopt a condescending attitude. He simply nodded and asked me to wait till he hunted around.

A week later he telephoned me and gave me a name and a telephone number. Vira Kheshvala, staying at two minutes distance – if one is a crow – and four minutes distance – if one is on a bike – from my residence, amazing!

"She does not like to speak about her knowledge or her powers. Also, she is very busy. She might even refuse you, so best of luck."

"What if she refuses?"

"We will try to get some other medium but I hope she sees you. She is very powerful, one of the best."

I read the name once again, Mrs Vira Kheshvala. I dialled her number.

"Hello...I...uh...I....wwwould like to speak with Mrs Vira..."

"Bai is not here. She will come on Tuesday. Somebody spoke in Marathi; which meant the family had gone out of town and this was a maid speaking.

I lit a cigarette and sighed. If only that soft, stubborn, tyrannical voice would let me meet...

"Will you stop cribbing and wait till Tuesday." The soft one spoke.

"Ahhhh yes."

For some reason, I could not make contact with Vira for another week. Then frustrated with everything, including my own lackadaisical attitude, I decided if I had to, I would phone all day but I would make contact with Vira. I got lucky.

"Mrs Vira ..."

"Yes, speaking..."

"Oh thank God...sorry I am...uh...Ruzbeh Bharucha and... uh...I am writing a book on spirit communication...life after death...and uh...I've heard that you are uh...I mean...a medium...I would like to meet you."

Not bad huh? Fluent, to the point, beautiful diction! There was silence at the other end. I had stopped breathing long since.

"I am not a very powerful medium...why don't you meet and speak to Mrs..."

"Believe me I can't..."

"Why not..."

"Uh...please can I meet you? I live very close to your house..."

"Where do you live?"

I told her and she seemed pleasantly surprised.

"Are you related to Eruch Bharucha... Darab Bharucha...?"

"Darab Bharucha was my grandfather and Eruch Bharucha was his brother, my dad's uncle...my grand-uncle." This seemed to make a great difference.

"I knew Eruch very well...Okay...come over, next week but give me a call before coming."

I thanked her profusely and sighed. At last I was going to meet a psychic; a medium who chit-chatted with spirits. But it took me another 10 days to find myself standing in front of Vira Kheshvala's door. It was opened by a lady, around 60 years of age, one of the most serene faces I have seen in my life, with a warm, soothing smile, twinkling eye and a welcoming voice.

"Ruzbeh? I'm Vira. You look very young to be interested in spirits. Please come in."

I do not know why, but for some reason I was not at all surprised to see Vira as a well-mannered, soft-spoken, immaculately dressed lady. In movies, whether Indian or international, I have seen psychics and mediums who are a strange amalgam of clowns and garish and ridiculously attired witches in a bad reproduction of Macbeth. Vira looked life a well-dressed housewife on a day out. I have seen her often now but have always been amazed at the serene look on her face, the warmth in her personality and a twinkle of joy in her eyes with a soft voice which often is even apologetic when she confesses that she is a medium; not by choice but by demands of fate.

I entered her cosy, well-done house and we sat on the small balcony that faced a playground where a game of football was in progress. A group of Zoroastrian boys played with a college team. The Zoroastrian boys were conspicuous by their appearances as well as the swear words each one had handy whenever he wanted to catch the attention of his team mate.

Vira inquired of my family. She knew them very well. Then she smiled and informed that she, her husband's side of the family, and I were related; yes, very far off but we certainly were related. Our blood had a link.

"I want to write a book about life after death and communication with spirits, basically a book on psychics, mediums, etc."

"But dear I am not the right person. I am not a very powerful medium..."

"No, no. Why don't you speak to her (the same famous medium). She is very powerful..."

"I know but something seems to be stopping me from meeting and speaking to her."

Surprisingly like my uncle, she too did not show any surprise; as though she was used to inquisitive voices making unreasonable demands. We heard a car honk and she stood up.

"I am terribly sorry but can you give me a call after four days. Let us see what we can do for you."

I reached home.

"Is it you or your spirit?" My family was filled with wise guys. "Back so soon? What happened? The spirit world wants nothing to do with you?"

"Your attempts at humour are commendable but Vira had to visit somebody at the hospital. She is a very nice person..."

"Wise too. She really got you out of the house real fast. Ha-ha."

I lay down, shut my eyes and inhaled deep. These guys! I turned and began to look at the diva which burned on the prayer table. All of a sudden my eyes rested on Sri Paramhansa Yogananda's Autobiography Of a Yogi. I got up quickly and picked up the well-thumbed book. I had read it first when I was 18. Given to me by my late uncle, Jamshed Guzdar, may God rest his soul in peace and may he make spiritual progress. I had re-read the book months earlier. I remembered that there was an entire chapter devoted to life after death. I leafed through the pages randomly and stopped at the Resurrection of Sri Swami Sri Yuketeswar Giri, the great guru of the author. I smiled and shut the book. Somebody up there was trying His level best to help me.

The first book that I read about God, the paranormal world, the world of yogis and mystics and life beyond was Sri Paramahansa Yogananda's *Autobiography of a Yogi*. It still remains my favourite. I am not the only person who seems to be fascinated by the book. The book was written by Sri Paramhansa Yogananda (January 5, 1893 to March 7, 1952) in 1946. Since then it has seen 13 editions (at last count) and has sold, I assume millions of copies. At present, the Autobiography of a Yogi is used in over 100 universities and colleges as required reading for courses in comparative religion, psychology, literature, philosophy, sociology and even biology. It obviously is not the venture of a mere mortal. The book has been divinely conceived and thus, naturally blessed.

To highlight the spiritual advancement of Sri Paramhansa Yogananda, I shall only reprint an extract of a letter from Mr. Harry T Rowe, Mortuary Director of Forest Lawn Memorial Park, Los Angeles (in which the body of Sri Paramhansa Yogananda was placed after the great master entered mahasamadhi).

Sri Paramhansa Yogananda entered mahasamadhi (a yogi's final conscious exit from the body) in Los Angeles, California on March 7, 1952, after concluding his speech at a banquet held in honour of Mr. BR Sen, the then Ambassador of India. The sage demonstrated the power of yoga not only in life but also in death. Weeks after His departure, Sri Paramhansa Yogananda's face shone with the divine lustre of incorruptibility. The letter by Mr. Rowe, Mortuary Director is as follows:

"The absence of any visual signs of decay in the dead body of Paramhansa Yogananda offers the most extraordinary case in our experience...no physical

49

disintegration was visible on his body even 20 days after death...no indication of mould was visible on his skin and no visible desiccation (drying up) took place in the bodily tissues. This state of perfect preservation of a body is, so far as we know from mortuary annals, an unparalleled one...no odour of decay emanated from his body at any time..."

"The physical appearance of Yogananda on March 27, just before the bronze cover of the casket was put into position, was the same as it had been on March 7. He looked as fresh and as unravaged by decay on March 27 as he had looked on the night of his death. On March 27, there was no reason to say that his body had suffered any visible physical disintegration at all. For these reasons we state again that the case of Paramhansa Yogananda is unique in our experience."

Sri Paramhansa Yogananda's guru was Sri Sri Swami Sri Yuketeswar Giri (1855-1936). I can only hope the reader has realised that if the student himself showed such a high degree of God consciousness even in death, then to what level of God consciousness must Sri Paramhansa Yogananda's guru himself have reached? Sri Sri Swami Sri Yuketeswar Giri, resurrected after three months of leaving his physical body. This chapter on the guru's resurrection is one of the most fascinating insights ever penned down regarding life after death. Sri Paramhansa Yogananda's guru though humble, kind, soft-hearted and wise was a stern and strict disciplinarian.

Sri Sri Swami Sri Yuketeswar Giri left his physical body on March 21, 1936. March 21, the day of spring equinox is an auspicious day in both the Hindu as well as the Zoroastrian calendar. The advent of spring, the blooming of flowers, buzzing of bees and the nuisance of Cupid; it is Navroz for Zoroastrians, the first day of the Persian New Year.

It was in the second week of June in the same year when Sri Paramhansa Yogananda saw the vision of Lord Krishna and described it as follows. "The divine figure waved to me, smiling and nodding in greeting. When I could not understand the exact message of Lord Krishna, He departed with a gesture of blessing. Wondrously uplifted, I felt that some spiritual event was presaged."

The spiritual event took place a week later in a Bombay hotel at 3 o'clock in the afternoon. Sri Paramhansa Yogananda was roused from His meditation by a beatific light and beheld in front Him, Sri Sri Swami Sri Yuketeswar Giri in flesh and blood. Naturally the meeting was emotional and for the first time Sri Paramhansa Yogananda did not bend to touch His guru's feet for blessings but embraced His master in such a tight embrace that the latter gave a mirthful chuckle and said: " Please dear one, won't you relax your hold a little?"

When an emotional Sri Paramhansa Yogananda inquired as to how His guru's body felt as real as when the great Master was on earth, the reply was: "This is a flesh and blood body. Though I see it as ethereal, to your sight it is physical. From cosmic atoms I created an entirely new body..."

This act of creating the body from atoms has been mentioned in a number of books. Enlightened beings can materialise their bodies by arranging atoms. Thus, by quick dematerialisation they can travel instantly from place to place, planet to planet or from one dimension to the other. This is also mentioned in the world renowned book *Aliens Amongst Us* by Ruth Montgomery.

According to Ruth Montgomery, an international best-selling author on paranormal literature, "The extra-terrestrials come and go at will because of their ability to disintegrate solids and reassemble them, wherever they wish. This is a law of the universe that is not yet fully understood on planet earth but it does not defy natural laws. They travel from other planetary systems to the earth plane by thought."

According to Sri Sri Swami Sri Yuketeswar Giri, the human soul is encased in three different bodies and so is the world of creation. "You have read in the scriptures," explained the master to Sri Paramhansa Yogananda, "that God encased the human soul successively in three bodies – the idea or causal body; the subtle astral body, seat of man's mental and emotional natures; and the gross material body. On earth, a man is equipped with his physical senses. An astral person works through his consciousness and feelings and a body made of *lifetrons*[1] or *prana*. (According to Hindu scriptures there is not only *anu*, "atom" and *paramanu*, "beyond the atom", finer electronic energies; but also *prana*, a creative *lifetronic* force.

Prana is intelligent life force. They guide embryonic development according to a karmic design. A causal-bodied being remains in the blissful realm of ideas. My work is with those astral devotees who are preparing to enter or re-enter the causal world."

According to Sri Sri Swami Sri Yuketeswar Giri, of the three bodies as well as three types of worlds, the causal is the most sublime. It is associated with thought, the idea. Thus, causal desires are fulfilled by perception alone.

In the causal world, the soul is encased in just one more body after which it can merge with God and be one with God Almighty. The important point to remember is that though the causal world and the causal body are the most sublime states of consciousness, the soul is still encased; it still has a body; thus it is still not in its original state of God-consciousness or awareness or presence. When the soul breaks through the causal body, it

---

1   *Lifetrons* is a word coined by Paramahansa Yogananda for *prana*

realises total freedom and final merger and union with God. After the causal stage, the soul is without any desire (body, emotion, and mind) and accepts with sheer perception that creation is a thought; a phenomenal idea of God and the soul itself is a part of the Great One, thus it is God too.

After death our soul enters the astral world, the second stage and the astral body thrives on vibrations. Emotions and feelings are predominant and reign supreme. (I sense danger, is the astral world dominated by women? Just an odd thought from a gross man.) In the astral world, the inhabitants enjoy ethereal (divine) music and are entranced by the sight of all creation as exhaustless expression of changing light.

The third world is the physical world. The inhabitants thrive on coke, Pepsi, blood and prefer in most cases gold to God. Needless to say according to the creation chart, the physical or gross world stinks.

Thus, not only is the soul encased in three bodies but also, there are three dimensions to it. The final aim of every soul is to break through each of these barriers and merge with God. Each world is besotted with temptations. The gross has so many that we would need another book just to get through half of the temptations lurking! The astral world is so ethereal and divine that the soul gets entrapped in such heavenly frills and forgets that to move towards God and achieve God consciousness is a must and our indulgence in pleasure of the senses is the real barrier for the final union with God.

"I am in truth resurrected not on earth but on an astral planet. It is called *Hiranyaloka* or Illumined *Astral Planet.* There I am aiding advanced beings to rid themselves of astral karma and thus attain liberation from astral rebirths. As prophets are sent on earth to help men work out their physical karma, so I have been directed by God to serve on an astral planet as a saviour," Sri Sri Swami Sri Yukateswar Giri informed his awestruck pupil.

Two things of importance: One is that *Hiranyaloka* is the highest planet for advanced astral souls. Thus, those on this planet who have passed through other astral planes and through many astral rebirths have reached *Hiranyaloka*.. Only after reaching *Hiranyaloka* can the soul hope to reach the causal world.

"The dwellers on Hiranyaloka are highly developed spiritually. All of them had acquired in their last incarnation on earth, the meditation given power of consciously leaving their physical bodies at death. No one can enter unless he or she had experienced during his or her previous terrestrial life, the states of *sabikalpa* and *nirbikalpa samadhi*."

The second important point I wish to make is equally philosophical. If no one can enter the causal world unless one has experienced during one's past terrestrial life the states of *sabikalpa* and *nirbikalpa samadhi*, then we guys here have a long way to go before *moksha*.

In *sabikalpa Samadhi*, the devotee has attained God realisation but can maintain this "only during a trance state" which is a state of meditation or prayer. While in *nirbikalpa Samadhi*, the devotee even moves about in the world without any loss of God-perception. (Saints are perpetually in this state.) Sri Sri Swami Sri Yuketeswar Giri further informed that even after reaching and realising these states of *samadhi* and after the soul drops its physical or terrestrial casing, it still cannot enter the causal world directly. Though these souls reach the topmost rung of the astral world, these souls still have certain astral karmas to work out.

"*Hiranyaloka* inhabitants have already passed through the ordinary astral spheres where nearly all beings from earth must go at death. There they destroy many seeds of karma connected with their past actions in astral worlds."

According to Sri Sri Swami Sri Yuketeswar Giri, only very advanced souls are able to work on their karmas effectively in the astral worlds. This is because most souls are so mesmerised and enchanted by the beauties and splendour of the astral worlds that they do not see the necessity for strenuous spiritual effort. But those souls who still work hard at moving closer to God are reborn in new astral bodies on *Hiranyaloka*, the astral sun or heaven where Sri Sri Swami Sri Yuketeswar Giri works as a saviour. If you are wondering how a soul takes rebirth in the astral and causal worlds, there is an explanation.

"No one is born of woman. Astral persons, through fiat (command) of their cosmically attuned will, bring an offspring into being in significantly patterned astral forms. A recently physically disembodied person arrives in an astral family by invitation, drawn by similar mental and spiritual tendencies." All this is fine, but how does death take place even after a soul has discarded its human shell on earth? Sri Sri Swami Sri Yuketeswar Giri further elaborates. "Physical death is attended by disappearance of breath and the disintegration of fleshy cells. Astral death consists of the dispersement of *lifetrons*, those manifest units of cosmic energy which constitute the bodily life of astral beings."

So let us assume a person dies and the soul reaches one of the many levels of the astral world. If the soul spends its time just enjoying itself and having an ethereal blast, once its time is up, it dies and in all probability it is reborn on earth to work out its karma.

"Experiencing astral death in due time, man thus passes from the consciousness of astral birth and death to that of physical birth and death. These recurrent cycles of astral and physical encasement are the ineluctable destiny of all unenlightened beings. Scriptural definitions of heaven and hell some times stir man's deeper-than-subconscious memories of his long series of experiences in the blithesome astral and disappointing terrestrial worlds."

I wondered how long the soul stays in the astral or causal worlds. Who decides that the time is right for either moving to the physical world or to higher planes? According to Sri Sri Swami Sri Yukteswar Giri, a person dwells on an astral plane depending upon the weight of one's material karma that draws the person back to the physical realm. Sometimes the physical desires are so forceful and demanding that after physical death, the soul immediately returns to earth. But usually the average length of time spent on the astral plane is 500 to 1000 years. "Just as sequoias outlive other trees by millenniums or, as yogis live for several hundred years though most men die before the age of 60, so also exceptional persons live on an astral plane for about 2000 years."

Astral beings do not have to face painful death. The astral world is free from disease, unwilling death and old age. Of course, astral death on high planets like *Hiranyaloka* is looked upon as liberation but that is only if the soul moves from *Hiranyaloka* to the causal world.

Rebirths not only take place from astral to physical but from causal to astral also. Even after the soul crosses over from *Hiranyaloka,* the topmost astral rung, to the causal world, the last cage of the soul after which the soul merges with God and becomes one with Him; it could, due to its yet lingering desires and karmas, take rebirth in *Hiranyaloka*. Thus, souls move from the causal world to the astral; from thought or idea to the world of emotion and vibration. The important point is that even after the soul has advanced and reached such a high stature it still craves. No wonder every religious book, every prophet, sage, master repeatedly warns us of the danger of attachment, desire and craving. The repercussions are felt not only on earth but in the spirit world too.

Apart from Sri Sri Swami Sri Yukteswar Giri, a number of authors on the spiritual have mentioned the importance of attaining a desireless state, which can be achieved only when the soul has realised the futility of nurturing desires. They stress upon the incalculable harm the soul does to its own self by constantly craving for either physical or vibratory pleasures whereas, its real craving should be for God and for merging in the infinite bliss that is God. But till the soul does not get rid of all the casings, physical, astral and causal, it cannot be free.

"My work is with those astral devotees who are preparing to enter or re-enter the causal world."

Now what are astral worlds like and how do its inhabitants go about life after physical death? According to Sri Sri Swami Sri Yuketeswar Giri, there are many astral worlds. As the soul moves ahead spiritually, the astral world it is born into is a higher, a more subtler and sublime plane than the previous one. The highest astral world or plane is *Hiranyaloka*. The ordinary astral plane is peopled with millions of astral beings who have arrived from earth. The astral world is not the base solely for mankind. According to Sri Sri Swami Sri Yuketeswar Giri, there are also different fairies, mermaids, goblins, gnomes, fish, animals as well as demigods and spirits, all residing on different astral planets, in accordance with their karmas. Evolved ones can travel freely, while those who are not as evolved are restricted to a limited zone. Astral folk use astral vehicles or masses of light to travel from place to place, planet to planet. Travel by use of light has been mentioned in a number of books. This mode has a number of advantages. It is faster than electricity or radioactive energies. One can traverse from planet to planet, between astral worlds, even through different dimensions, in moments. The most important advantage is that astral beings do not have to deal with any Municipal Corporation, the department which is filled with aspiring archaeologists whose sole aim and yearning in life is to dig up roads, forget about them and let nature take its bumpy course.

What is the astral universe made up of? According to Sri Sri Swami Sri Yuketeswar Giri, the astral universe is made of subtle vibrations of light and colour. It is hundreds of times larger than the material world. There are countless astral solar and stellar systems. The astral suns and moons are lovelier than those found in the physical universe. The days and nights are longer. The environmentalists can heave a sigh of relief and be informed by a number of authors on the paranormal, that the astral universe is infinitely beautiful, clean, pure and orderly. There are no barren lands or terrestrial blemishes like weeds bacteria, insects, snakes, politicians, etc. Also there is no change of season. "The astral spheres maintain an even temperature of an eternal spring with occasional luminous white snow and rain of multi-coloured light. Astral worlds abound in opal lakes and bright seas and Rainbow Rivers."

Fallen angels or souls dwell in the dark lower regions of the astral cosmos. If they work out their karma, then progression is possible.

"Astral beings dematerialise and materialise their forms at will. Flowers or fish or animals can metamorphose themselves for a time into astral men. All astral beings are free to assume any form. Also, everything is possible by just willing or feeling intensely and communication is conducted through telepathy and astral television. Unlike the three-dimensional physical world cognised by the five senses, the astral spheres are perceptible to the all-inclusive sixth-sense, intuition – though astral people have all the outer sensory organs and skin but employ the intuitional sense to experience sensations through any part of the body. They can see through the ear or nose or skin, hear through the eyes or tongue."

The astral world is not as gross as the physical universe but not as subtle as the causal cosmos thus, the diet of astral inhabitants too is different.

"Luminous ray-like vegetables abound in the astral soils. Astral world dwellers consume fruits and vegetables and drink nectar that flows from glorious fountains of light and in astral brooks and rivers. Just as the ordinary invisible images of men on earth can be summoned from the ether and made visible by a television device, later being dismissed into space...in the same way immense gardens may be materialised, returning later to etheric invisibility." *Hirayanloka* dwellers, being closer to the causal world are almost freed from the necessity of eating.

According to Sri Sri Swami Sri Yuketeswar Giri as well as other authors, psychics and clairvoyants, the astral body resembles the exact counterpart of that when the person was on earth. The astral people look younger, healthier and devoid of deformities and pain. Usually the person looks similar when he or she was young on earth but in the end it solely depends on each individual. For example, Sri Sri Swami Sri Yuketeswar Giri preferred to keep His appearance exactly as His last physical form on earth, that of an old but nonetheless healthy man.

What has been bothering me since I got involved with this book and after communicating with psychics was that as each of us has lived innumerable lives, how does one recognise family and friends of different earlier lives? A person may remember everything of his recently concluded earthly sojourn but would he remember his family of his other incarnations?

"Friends of other lives easily recognise one another in the astral world. Rejoicing at the immortality of friendship, they realise the indestructibility of love, often doubted at the time of the sad, delusive parting of earthly life. An astral person meets a multitude of relatives, fathers, mothers, wives, husbands, children and friends acquired during different incarnations on earth, as they appear from time to time in various parts of the astral cosmos. Though the outward appearance of loved ones may have changed, an astral world resident employs his unerring intuition to recognise all those once dear to him on other planes of existence and welcomes them to their new astral home. Because each atom in creation is inextinguishably showered with individuality, an astral friend will be recognised by others no matter what costume he may don..."

The Bhagawad Gita VII: 4 states: "The eight elemental qualities that enter into all created life from atom to man are earth, water, fire, air, ether, motion, mind and individuality" which means that each one of us is a separate individual, though a part of God. That in each one of us burns not only the spark of God but also the spark of our own individuality. The most important point I have learnt is that even after the soul breaks free of its causal body and is a free soul which has merged with God; it still retains its individuality. No wonder sages and religious texts, all repeat over and over again that not only is the individual responsible for his or her karma but also that each soul is a part of God, thus each soul is God itself and that we all are immortal too. The soul is immortal thus, the individual soul merged with God too is immortal; just like a wave is a separate identity yet it is a part of the ocean. It merges with the ocean and once again comes to the shore as an independent identity.

The causal world is the last stage after which the soul eventually becomes once again free from any body or cage to unite with God. To achieve *moksha*, the final freedom may take thousands of years and countless reincarnations but ironically, according to Sri Sri Swami Sri Yuketeswar Giri, "Man as an individualised soul is essentially causal bodied. The body is a matrix of the 35 ideas required by God as the basic or causal thought forces from which He later formed the subtle astral body of 19 elements and the gross physical body of 16 elements."

The causal body can materialise anything and everything in sheer thought. "Causal beings consider the enjoyment of physical sensations or astral delights in terms of vibrations as gross and suffocating to the soul's fine sensibilities. Causal beings work out their desires by materialising them instantly. Those who find themselves covered only by the delicate veil of the causal body can bring universes into manifestation even as does the Creator. Because all creation is made up of the cosmic dream-texture, the soul thinly clothed in the causal has vast realisation of power."

Apart from Sri Sri Swami Sri Yuketeswar Giri, a number of authors on the paranormal have mentioned the importance of a desireless state, which can be achieved only when a person has realised the futility of nurturing desires; the harm it does to its own self by constantly craving for either physical or vibratory pleasures and that its real craving should be for God and merging in the infinite bliss that is God. But till the soul does not get rid of all the casings namely physical, astral and causal, it cannot be free.

Coming back to the causal world, how do its inhabitants go about their life? Perfect masters, psychics, religious texts, all insist that for the normal human being it is impossible to visualise and grasp the causal world. According to Sri Sri Swami Sri Yuketeswar Giri: "In order to understand it, one would have to possess such tremendous powers of concentration that he could close his eyes and visualise the astral cosmos and the physical cosmos in all their vastness as existing in ideas only.... if one succeeded in converting or resolving the two cosmoses with all their complexities into sheer ideas, he would then reach the causal world and stand on the borderline of fusion between mind and matter. There one perceives all created things, solids, liquids, gases, electricity, energy, all beings, Gods, men, animals, plants, and bacteria as forms of consciousness, just as a man can close his eyes and realise that he exists, even though his body is invisible to his physical eyes and is present only as an idea."

The causal world is the last stage, the last body that cages the soul, preventing it from achieving freedom and a reunion with

God, our Omnipotent Father. It is the world where thought, the idea, is the essence and the only truth. Hence, the realisation dawns and is accepted that all that one has seen and perceived, planets and different dimensions are only "in reality created from the minutest particles of God-thought chopped and divided by Maya, the law of relativity that apparently intervenes to separate creation from its creator."

Thus, in the causal world thought-beings exist and souls can recognise one another as individualised points or thoughts of joyous spirits. "Causal beings by thought alone are able to see, hear, smell, taste and touch: they create anything or dissolve it by the power of the cosmic mind."

Even in the causal world there exist death and re-birth but they too are thought-based; as the soul has no body but just the thought of its existence. Naturally, unlike the physical and astral worlds, the diet in the causal world is different. The thought reigning supreme and "the causal-bodied beings feast only on the ambrosia of eternally new knowledge. They drink from the springs of peace, roam on the trackless soil of perception, swim in the ocean...endlessness of bliss. Lo! See their bright thought-bodies zoom past trillions of spirit-created planets, fresh bubbles of universes, wisdom-stars, spectral dreams of golden nebulae on the sky bosom of Infinity."

After death and re-birth in the causal world which could itself take thousands of years, the soul by deeper ecstasies withdraws itself from its causal body or thought and puts on the vastness of the causal ocean where it merges in the "One Cosmic Ocean with all its waves – eternal laughter, thrills, and throbs."

But a point to be remembered and which needs repeated assertion is that even after the soul sheds all its bodies and merges with God Infinite and becomes a free soul, no longer in the clutches of births, deaths, rebirths, away from karma, the soul still retains its individuality. Once the soul escapes from the law of karma, it no longer needs to undergo incarnations but may still decide to incarnate in either of the three worlds; physical, astral, causal; to help other souls move towards the final *moksha*.

"A master who achieves this final freedom may elect to return to earth as a Prophet to bring other human beings back to God or like myself, he may choose to reside in the astral cosmos. There, a saviour assumes some of the burden of the inhabitants' karma and thus helps them terminate their cycle of reincarnation in the astral cosmos and go on permanently to the causal spheres. Or, a freed soul may enter the causal world to aid its beings to shorten their span in the causal body and thus attain Absolute Freedom."

The last question Sri Paramhansa Yogananda asked of his guru, regarding the karma that forces souls to return to the three worlds and the answer of Sri Sri Swami Sri Yuketeswar Giri, sum up the chapter beautifully.

"The physical karma or desires of man must be completely worked out before his permanent stay in astral worlds becomes possible. Two kinds of beings live in the astral spheres. Those who still have earthly karma to dispose of and who must therefore re-inhabit a gross physical body in order to pay their karmic debts, may be classified after physical death, as temporary visitors to the astral world rather than as permanent residents.

"Beings with unredeemed earthly karma are not permitted after astral death to go to the high causal sphere of cosmic ideas, but must shuttle to and fro between the physical and astral worlds only, conscious successively of their physical body of 16 gross elements and their astral body of 19 subtle elements. After each loss of his physical body, however, an undeveloped being from the earth remains for the most part in the deep stupor of the death-sleep and is hardly conscious of the beautiful astral sphere. After the astral rest, such a man returns to the material plane for further lessons, gradually accustoming himself, through repeated journeys to the worlds of subtle astral texture."

"Long-established residents of the astral universe, on the other hand, are those who, freed forever from all material longings, need return no more to the gross vibrations of earth. Such beings have only astral and causal karma to work out. At astral death these beings pass into the infinitely finer and more delicate causal world. At the end of a certain span, determined by cosmic law, these advanced beings then return to *Hiranyaloka* or a similar high astral planet, reborn in a new astral body to work out their unredeemed astral karmas. My son, you may now comprehend more fully that I am resurrected by divine decree as a saviour of astrally reincarnating souls coming back from the causal sphere, in particular, rather than of those astral beings who are coming up from the earth. Those from the earth, if they still retain vestiges of material karma, do not rise to the very high astral planets like *Hiranyaloka*."

"Just as most people on earth have not learnt through meditation-acquired vision to appreciate the superior joys and advantages of astral life and thus, after death, desire to return to the limited, imperfect pleasures of earth, many astral bodies fail to picture the advanced state of spiritual joy in the causal world and dwelling on thoughts of the more gross and gaudy astral happiness, yearn to revisit the astral paradise. Heavy astral karma must be redeemed by such beings before they can achieve after astral death, a permanent stay in the causal thought-world, so thinly partitioned from the Creator."

"Only when a being has no further desires for experiences in the pleasing-to-the-eye astral cosmos and cannot be tempted to go back there, does he remain in the causal world. Completing the work of redeeming all causal karma or seeds of past desires, the confined soul thrusts out the last of the three corks of ignorance and emerging from the final jar of the causal body, co-mingles with the Eternal."

The Autobiography of a Yogi is a fascinating book, humorous and well written. It was my first and as I mentioned earlier, still remains my favourite book on the life beyond, the power of the mind and the all-pervading importance of yoga. If you have not read the book then I suggest you do so immediately.

After finishing work on this chapter, I sighed and once again picked up the phone, hoping Vira would see me again the next day.

I sat once again on the familiar balcony. Vira sat in front of me, leafing through a few notes.

"I don't think I mentioned this earlier, but I communicate with Meher Baba. The first time you came I was not sure whether I should speak to you freely and whether you are serious about the topic of life after death or not. You seem to be too young for all this. But after you left, the next morning when I sat down to pray, I was informed by Meher Baba that you are genuine in your search for this knowledge and that you have been sent by Him specially for a book, they want you to write and want me and my friends to help you get the book published."

I shifted uncomfortably in my chair. Even my mother (supposedly a boy's best friend) would be hard pressed for words in support of her son whose life has been erratic and apparently rudderless. To call me genuine (in anything) was taking spiritual love for all a little too far.

"Meher Baba has told me to inform you that He has sent you here specially; and that is why, though you wanted to go to someone else, something kept stopping you."

Though I had heard of Meher Baba and had seen His photograph in the clinic of my children's gynaecologist-cum-GP and an ardent Meher Baba devotee, Mehru Vaghchhuipwalla, I did not know much about the great Sage.

"How did Meher Baba enter your life and how does He speak to you?" A reasonable question to start this most profound of subjects, I thought. It seemed most natural to talk about these matters with Vira whose integrity I did not doubt even for a moment. As most of those close to me shall vouch, I go more

66

by my gut feelings than the dictates of my grey cells; a method that has always helped me in a true assessment of people. Further, Vira did not charge money to help people; she shied away from publicity; she had not once allowed any journalist to interview her and mainly she wanted to lead a private life. Vira Kheshvala, like many of her psychic brethren, lived a life away from the gloss and glamour associated with this esoteric talent.

"I will tell you in brief how I became a 'so-called' medium."

Though a mother of three girls herself, Vira still loved her niece, Cheherazade, dearly. Cheherazade was like a daughter to her, Cheherazade and Ketu (daughter of Amy, the clairvoyant) both expired in an Air-India crash on January 1, 1978. Cheherazade, a young beautiful girl, full of life, was working as an airhostess with Air-India; she boarded the ill-fated flight after having met and wished her family a Happy New Year. The aircraft crashed into the sea shortly after takeoff due to the failure of an important instrument in low visibility conditions and failure of the flight crew to make use of other functioning instruments to determine their flight attitude.

Their deaths affected the family in a way that words can never describe. Two beautiful girls had been snatched away by a seemingly nonchalant Providence in the prime of their youth, when life was just beginning to take on colours of the rainbow and the world seeming a nice place to be in and enjoy. A phase that was ideal; just after confusing adolescence ends and before responsibilities set up shop in one's life.

For a long time, Vira lived in state of unceasing sorrow. It was hard for her to accept that someone as young as Cheherazade had been snatched away by God in so cruel a manner. She prayed for the young girl's soul to rest in peace. Then once in a while she began to see Cheherazade in her dreams. A smiling Cheherazade would console and comfort Vira. Of course, Vira did not give the dreams importance. She took it as a sub-conscious mind grieving for a beloved niece.

"I thought these dreams were my sub-conscious mind working overtime. Not once did I think that Cheherazade was trying to communicate with me. I mean I had never believed in psychics and mediums."

A few weeks later a friend of Vira's arrived and inquired if Vira believed in communicating with spirits of those who had died.

"I never believed in all these things. We were always taught and told that our religion was against disturbing our dead family members. We were told that spirits go through a lot of trouble, pain and discomfort when they are called to speak to their loved ones. Thus, when this friend talked about spirits, at first I wanted to have nothing to do with all this. But after a while the friend informed me that a spirit of a young girl who had died recently in an air crash had contacted her group through the planchette and wanted to speak to her family; specially her aunt. Believe me; I did not know what a planchette was and how spirits communicated. But I knew the girl was none other than my Cheherazade. I agreed, I was desperate to hear from her and just know that she was all right."

The medium who had received the message from the spirit world was Phiroze Kapadia. This gentle and noble psychic's reputation was already established in the India metaphysical world. Phiroze Kapadia and his wife Arnavaz Kapadia, a powerful psychic herself, have played a great role in moulding Vira into a medium. Phiroze, before mental exhaustion made him virtually unaware of his surroundings, was a dynamic psychic leader. Even Meher Baba and Guru Nanak repeatedly mention Phiroze's contribution to psychic awareness as well as training most of the prominent psychics in Mumbai, including Vira Keshvala.

"Phiroze has introduced so many of us into this field that for most of us he is our guru. Unfortunately since 1997, after an operation, the co-ordination of his mind with other sensory inputs has been affected. Though he is present, he seems to be in another world. He was really a very powerful and a great medium. He used to go into a trance and a monk used to give lectures on all these subjects through Phiroze. The monk is his Guide."

That day, Cheherazade communicated with Vira through the planchette. It was here that Cheherazade revealed to Vira that she used to frequent her (Vira) while she slept.

"When I asked her what was the cause of the crash she refused to divulge anything. She kept saying that it was over, it was destiny and that we should all keep the incident behind us. She kept telling us that she liked to communicate with us."

"You see, we were brain-washed by our elders and our so-called enlightened people that there was nothing like communication with spirits. That all this was hocus-pocus, that it was indulged in by those who wanted to fool people and make easy money. But Phiroze never took a rupee from anyone; secondly, the things that Cheherazade divulged to us were so intimate that no one but Cheherazade and we, her immediate family, could have known. So slowly I began to attend more séances and saw how communication was done through automatic writing, trance etc."

It took some time for Vira to be comfortable with the fact that she was getting drawn into a world she was initially told existed in the minds of cranks and frauds. Or even if spirit communication was possible then the spirits were being forced to do so against their will. That it was a sin as it was causing discomfort and pain to the spirits being beckoned. Slowly, she began to separate the grain from the chaff.

"When did you begin to communicate on your own?"

"One day in my farmhouse in Karjat, a lovely place very close to Bombay, I sat down to pray. On the prayer table there was a painting of Zarathustra, a photograph of Cheherazade and a diva, a flame that burns in a vessel filled with oil or ghee. I was saying our Avesta prayers when I thought it was a trick of light but as I concentrated harder, I saw something in her throat move. At first I did not believe my eyes but when her throat throbbed as though with life again and again, I was certain that Cheherazade wanted to speak to me. I snatched a paper and held it the way I had seen mediums in automatic writing sessions hold a writing instrument. You know what automatic writing is, of course?"

I shook my head, for a man who wanted to write a book on the paranormal world I was amazingly ill-informed. According to Vira, in auto-writing, the medium holds a pen with a very light grip. So lightly that he or she cannot move it on his or her own. Then the medium concentrates on his or her Guide or Guardian Angel. The pen begins to move on its own. The spirit jots down messages through the pen. The writing style changes, the pressure, speed all differ from one's usual style of writing. The only danger is that sometimes the sub-conscious mind takes over and the person, who is acting as a medium, scribbles his or her own thoughts at rapid pace on the paper. Therefore, the mind is to be kept blank and concentration firm.

Vira held the pen lightly and stared with intent at Cheherazade's photograph. She then softly beseeched her niece that she should communicate with her through the pen.

"Then it happened. The pen moved on its own free will and Cheherazade wrote Hi Vira aunty; it was one of the most unforgettable moments of my life."

"Not many believed me that it was really Cheherazade writing. Nor did I at first. It took some time for my family and friends to be convinced. Of course, many times I too doubted myself."

To a person sitting opposite the medium, automatic writing does not appear to even remotely resemble anything paranormal. The pen moves in the usual way. It does not float or dance and go about its mystical job. The process looks so normal and mundane that the onlooker assumes that the medium is taking him or her for a jolly good ride. It is only when the pen begins to divulge intimate facts or usual mode of dialect, like a deceased wife scribbling, "Why you good for nothing goat" that the truth rings home.

"Have you kept all the communications with Cheherazade?" I inquired hopefully.

"I have my doubts but let me see, a few diaries may still be around. I will try and search them for you."

Six months later one lazy afternoon, on the advice of Meher Baba, Vira sat for the first time in a trance, to be the medium for Meher Baba to answer many questions put forward by an unemployed editor. Before the trance, Vira, Meher Castillino and Shiraz, Vira's daughter and I sat for a lengthy conversation, peppered with lots of gossip…what do you expect with three brilliant women and an unemployed author? It was Shiraz who really encouraged me and was certain that this book project would come through. Vira, after more probing, got me the above mentioned diaries and I have reprinted the material which I felt will give the reader an idea of the origin of Vira Kheshvala's growth as a psychic medium. Some names are not spelt out so as to respect their privacy.

I reprint from the diary and in Vira's own words:

Cheherazade and Ketu expired in an Air-India crash on January 1, 1978. The first recorded planchette session took place on Marc 31, 1978. It is given as follows:

What is your name?
Cheherazade.
What is your mother's name?
Gahver.
One person in this meeting you love a lot?

Auntu K....

Cheherazade, do you like it there without us?

Slowly

Who came to receive you at the other end?

Granny

Is Ketu with you?

Yes

F... saw you the other day. Does it mean anything? Is his life in danger?

No. I am near you all and him. I get the flowers and enjoy. Now that you   have seen me I won't appear again because we meet here.

Have you met Minoo uncle?

Yes. He is very sorry to see us in this world.

Why don't you come in my dreams? (Mother inquiring.)

Yes mamma I will try.

Daddy is very upset and he wants to meet you. He has no wish to live.

I know mamma. Convey to him that I have left this world for further study.

What do you feel when we pray?

I get satisfaction and he (her father) feels my presence.

Do you have any message for anyone?

Not at present. I will be in peace for some time and then I will be in a mood. Minoo uncle is staying with me.

Are you happy?

Of course

Without you I want to end my life soon, to die and be with you.

Please for my papa's sake, you have to live. Mamma, nobody is allowed to go against time.

Once when I was praying I heard my name "Auntu" being called out? (Khorshed)

I am glad to know you heard. I tried many times to make you all feel my presence.

Do you meet the other crew members? (Those who died in the air crash.)

We meet them often.

Do you stay with Ketu?

Yes, we stay together.

Any message for Faranak or Furi? (Vira's two elder daughters, cousin sisters of Cheherazade.)

Pinch you. (Some code between the cousins.) Do you remember ice-cream?

Do you and Ketu go along with Faranak on her flights?

(Faranak too is an air-hostess like Cheherazde and Ketu), will you both accompany her on her Mauritius flight?

Yes enjoy everybody. I am very happy mamma. (Cheherazade left and then Ketu gave the following message.)

My love to all my pets. Tell mummy that I am progressing and I will help her about her health. I want to see her happy. God is great. My love, bye-bye my people we are one.

Cheherazade in between sent the following message to Vira.

I like your guide, her name is Sussano. She is about my height. (With this message Cheherazade confirmed Vira's apparition of the Nun's form she had seen at her first séance. She had not yet seen her face though).

Communication held on May 13, 1978

Kindly give your name?

I am Cheherazade, happy to see you.

What is your world like?

Same as yours

Do you like it?

Yes, I am getting used to it.

It is better than this world?

Well, can't say.

We cannot see you.

I will try in dreams.

Do you come in our dreams?

Yes

We do not remember seeing you.

I come

How do you pass your time? Are you studying anything?

Because I am new, I am not doing any particular work or studying as yet. Let me think of my own experience.

What experience?

Experience all around, then I will tell you.

How are you?

I am better now. I am happy because I can see you.

What plane are you on?

Fifth plane. (According to most psychics there are seven planes with innumerable sub-strata. It is presumed that the astral world has six planes with innumerable spheres in each plane and the seventh plane is the causal plane after which the soul merges with God).

Were you present on Y…'s birthday in the morning and evening?

Yes, why are you silent? You must not be sorry and shed tears; you too mamma. I feel when I see you weep. Now we have to follow God's wish.

Can we help you fulfil any of your wishes?

Not necessary at present.

Is M…. uncle with you today?

Yes, I told him to come with me.

Is he happy?

Yes

Does he want to convey any message to Khorshe aunty?

He says he comes and blesses you (Khorshed) every morning between 8 & 9. He says nothing will happen. S…. can't do any wrong (to Khorshed). He (M….) is behind you to protect you. Don't worry.

Do you meet A… or P…?

Yes once; they are sorry for me joining them.

Cheherazade darling, can you use your spiritual power to show yourself to Mummy?

When I get power I will appear. Both have to have power.

How is your granny?

Happy

Do you meet?

Yes

Do you show yourself to "Khorshed Aunty is glimpses?"

Twice only, I am glad.

Do you wish us to continue contacting you?

Yes

Are we hindering your progress?

Mamma, I tell you no one can hinder our progress now.

I always think of you; feel you. (Vira)

Your prayers are a help to me.

In what way does it help you?

I get mental peace. I dropped a flower when you were praying. I am really happy to hear that you could feel my presence.

Wait for us darling. Don't go away.

Yes, don't worry mamma.

How many planes are there?

Seven, the lowest is the first. Please take care of mamma. She does not eat properly.

Any message for A....uncle?

Everyone feels my absence but what can I do.

Any message for Mummy's birthday?

Hearty love, I will kiss her.

Do you come daily?

Yes

Anytime?

During lunch

Give us some indication when you come.

It will take time.

Is Ketu with you?

Yes, any message?

Give her my love. What do you and M....uncle do?

I play with him; run with him.

Met E....uncle?

Yes

Can you come direct?

Yes

Met my mummy? (Vira)

Yes, sixth plane. I am trying to concentrate upon God only so that I can get more power.

Can you come to London?

Yes, I will be with you.

Any message for auntu?

Continue reading books.

Were you with Faranak in Mauritius?

No, she only dreamt.

Any message for Dadu?

He is depressed, I feel it. He should not get worried. I am happy. His mind is over-controlled. I am praying for his mental peace.

Any message for Z….aunty?

Give company to dear mamma.

When should we contact you again?

After two months.

M….uncle?

After two months.

Do you want to go?

Yes

Keep yourself well.

My love to you all, bye-bye.

Communication date not recorded, in all probability two months after the above date

Please give your name.

I am Cheherazade.

Give some indication or identification to show you are there.

I try my best to touch, but could not. Power is not there.

Whose?

Mine

My love, how are you?

Mamma, I am quite happy now. I met you this morning.

When?

Seven to eight, while (you were) praying.

Are you happy to come or it is troublesome for you to do so?

I am very happy to come.

How do you pass your time?

Well, I am not given any work.

What do you do the whole day?

Khorshed aunty, I am helping newcomers, I like it.

Do our prayers help you and in what way?

Certainly, I get consolation. I pray for your mental peace, mamma.

Daddu is organising four memorial lectures in your memory at Cama Institute. Were you present at the Hall when the lectures were being held?

Yes

Liked it?

Yes

Have you any suggestion to make regarding the same?

No

What type of world are you living now in? Please give some information for our guidance.

Our world is vast and very complicated for newcomers. We have gardens, flowers of gold, changing like the sunshine. We sit there for hours together.

Do you have houses to stay in?

Yes, houses are made of invisible particles.

With whom are you staying?

We all are together now.

The crew?

Yes

Minoo uncle?

Yes

Granny?

She is on the sixth plane.

Do you meet D....aunty?

Sometimes we meet. When we feel tired we go in air lines and enjoy ourselves.

Will you be present for the birthday celebrations?

I enjoy with you, all and every function.

Will you be there to receive me when I come there or will you be gone to some other place? (Mummy).

I will be there to receive you.

Call us away. We want to be with you.

Don't say so. You have to do your duties for the family.

Call us Cheherazade soon?

No

Where is the astral world? How far away from here?

Very far away, we can fly anywhere as our body is very light; without flesh and blood.

Do you send messages on Saturday meetings? We are not convinced.

Yes, I am sending them but she may not understand my thoughts. My sweet Shiraz, be cheerful with my mamma. Auntu, your precious M….uncle is in touch with you. Tell Y…that I have gone for further study of a new world. Sure will help in exams.

Did you come as a warning for Faranak?

Yes

Was she in danger?

Yes, now danger is gone, do not worry.

Is Fluffy with you?

No

Ketu?

Yes

F….?

Yes

Are animals there?

Their plane is different.

Was there any connection between you and Ketu in your last life?

I don't know about the connection. I am tired now; my love to you all, bye-bye.

When shall we call you again?

After two months.

The questions of this communication are missing so I have only let those answers remain where the meaning becomes obvious. This communication must have taken place during late 1978 or early 1979.

I am Cheherazade. I am extremely pleased to see you all together…though I feel (sad) sometimes but we have to follow His rules, so we must not be sorry. My Guide explains to me everything so I am happy now. Yes Mamma, we (granny and I) meet often. Granny is on the sixth plane. M…uncle is near us every morning. Why don't you kiss me every morning? I love you all. Mamma how can I fail, I will come to you whenever you remember. We, (Ketu and Cheherazde), pray two to three times and meet in the garden; very beautiful garden, fine weather. I come to see you all anytime I like….I am very particular about my duties….I come with permission…(prayers) help to progress…(give) mental peace. Ketu is jolly here so she says no use crying. (I cry) sometimes. She (Ketu) will write morning 8 to 9. I will try. I will accompany Mamma. Please no tears mamma. I feel well; tell him (dad) that I have gone for further studies. Hearty love. I am happy. Love is same. We will meet…(next contact) three months… we smell only. Our body is without blood and flesh so we smell only. Invisible particles. I am happy. Love makes us happy and sorry (for the accident)…(when sad) think of God. (Ketu) gives her love to you all; my love to you all. Bye-bye till we meet again.

This meeting was held on April 12, 1979 at Mrs Rishi's residence.

Mr. and Mrs Rishi were among the founding psychic mediums and extremely powerful and committed. Mrs Rishi expired in early 1998. She came on the planchette and communicated with Vira. One of the things she revealed was that Phiroze Kapadia was present in astral form for her cremation. The amazing thing was that Phiroze Kapadia was virtually unaware of his surroundings because he had over-taxed his mind in trying to help people with paranormal activities. On the day and time Mrs Rishi was cremated, Phiroze was at this residence seemingly asleep. Mrs Rishi thanked Phoroze for paying his respects to her body in the astral form.

Name?
I am Cheherazade.
How are you?
I am pleased to see you all. I tried to appear in your dreams.
Whose?
Mamma's
I can't see you?
Yes I can see you all… I am quite alright.
What do you do?
What can I do? I pray to God for you (mother's) mental peace.
Give us an idea of your world?
I am getting used to it now. Our world is vast.
With whom are you staying?
Aunty I cannot stay alone. Grandpa meets me often.
Where is M….uncle?
Fifth plane.

Does Ketu meet you?

Very often we meet.

How do you pass your time?

I am not given any work here. I can pass time…I concentrate upon God.

The message sent for N… What was it?

I tried once. I was thinking you all and I could meet.

Are we hindering your progress by contacting you?

No mamma, none can hinder my progress. Try to write between seven and eight in the morning.

Message for Daddu?

Love is forever. What more can I say?

It was my fate. It is our destiny?

Yes

You want anything special to eat (on birthday)?

Ice cream

Mangoes?

I can smell only.

Is there any similarity between your life and our life?

Yes, we cannot eat but smell (only).

Is your body the same?

Yes, but without flesh and blood.

Will you be there when I come?

I don't know but I will be here till you meet me. Give my love to Shiraz (the youngest daughter of Vira). I have a guide here. He gives me lessons on how to progress and how to behave here. We progress on our own through prayers. It's a simple life. I am fond of clothes, that's why I told you to keep my clothes. I see only….It pained me because you are not using your clothes for my sake. You must use them. I will be happy.

M….uncle is happy to see you. He prays for you (M's wife).

He wants to see you happy. Whenever he likes, he comes to see you. He said no tears wanted. Please, he says he is always responding to your call. Why do you worry? He is protecting you.

Tell her (Faranak…daughter of Vira) I have come to this world for further studies.

Do you meet M often?

We meet often, don't worry. He is showing a wristwatch to you, his own. You must use it. How nice.

How come I do not feel your presence?

Go on trying (mamma) and I will make you feel my presence. I come in your dreams but you do not remember. What can I do? I will try to make my presence felt, difficult but I will try.

K….aunty I will speak in your ears. Concentrate when you sit for   prayers. I will try to whisper. Puri, look after my mamma.

When can we contact you again?

After two months… My love is very thick and strong.

Do you like it there?

No question of liking when we have to stay wherever we are. It is God's will, what more can I say. It is not in our hands… we can stay together but pray according to our own religion. …I say we have no books…concentrate on me and M uncle. Enough now; I will come with you home (mamma) and then go to my place. My love and kisses to you all. Bye-bye.

Communication On October 9, 1979

My beloved darling, how are you?

I am Cheherazade. I am very happy to see you here. I am better mamma.

How do you pass your time?

I help newcomers.

We think of you all the time and wonder what you are doing?

I am telling you that I help newcomers in my world.

Were you happy to come?

Yes

Are you now well settled in your new life?

Yes. I am getting used to it now. My guide gives lessons on how to behave and progress here.

In what way do you progress?

I get peace.

Do you wish to convey any message for Daddu?

I love Daddu. Prayers are very helpful to us. I like flowers.

Did you meet D…aunty?

Yes

Did she convey any message to you?

I did not ask her for any message. I told her that I communicate with mamma so why didn't she also come with me? Well, all of us are together so we can enjoy.

How is granny? Where is she?

She is not so keen to come. She said she enjoys her life but she loves you all. She cannot forget her dearest.

Do you come to our house sometimes? When?

Yes, when you pray in the morning. You must pray every morning, mamma. I will be with you.

Is there any religion there?

We pray according to our own religion.

Is there anything like time there?

Yes. We use the sand watch.

Any message for Sheraz?

She looks lovely. Sheraz, study. You will study. I like her.

Any message for Faranak?

Tell her to wear Sudra. Mamma, you must press her to wear it.

How is Ketu? Any message from her?

She is very happy and she does not like to come back. I mean rebirth, because she will forget you all.

Any message from M…?

He says he is as before but cannot appear before you so he feels it, but he is protecting you.

The house is dull without you my love.

You must not think so mamma. Take care of Daddy. I love to see you kissing my clothes.

Will you be there to receive us when we come there?

I feel better seeing you all. By God's grace I am happy. If God permits, I will stay till you all come. We, Ketu and I meet every morning and pray for your mental peace.

Where do you stay?

We stay together on the fifth plane. I don't know A's and F's plane.

Who goes to heaven?

That depends on one's character. I don't know if hell has any planes.

In what way should I (K) progress?

You should read books about our world. You will get more power. You should not lie down when you read. For developing power you should sit up and read. Mentally concentrate.

Will you contact me?

I will try my best to make you feel my presence. I am trying. Do you remember I dropped a rose when you were praying (K) aunty last week?

Daddy feels very low without you. Why don't you appear in his dreams?

I know mamma. I am trying.

Why did you not go to London when you were called? Was she powerful?

We were standing behind her. I think so. She was looking at us. M uncle in full dress. Your granny and grandpa also came.

When should we meet again?

After two months. I kiss you all. Bye-bye.

This conversation took place on February 7, 1980. More than two years had elapsed since the plane crash.

Love, give your name.

Cheherazade. I am happy to see you all. I was near you mummy and K aunty feels my presence at home; mornings eight to nine.

How are you? Do you think of us all the time as we do?

If I will be thinking of your world all the time I will not progress, my guide said. He said that I can go and see my dear ones any time but I must attend to my duties here also. Study how to concentrate upon God who is the power behind everything. So I am under the guidance of my Guide. I am quite happy. I can see you all. I come to kiss you before you go to bed (mamma). I love him (Daddy) and you also of course, I am with you. I am progressing and helping newcomers…those who are in need to be guided. They feel puzzled like me. So I like this work. I am doing it with permission of my guide who is very, very old.

Did you meet Dasturji D?

Once only

Did you meet K who has also gone to your world?

No, I don't go anywhere. I am on the fifth plane.

Where is your world? Tell us something about it.

Far away, but our body is so light that we can fly in the air within minutes.

If we could see you now… can we recognise you or have you changed in appearance considerably?

Same in appearance, counterpart of my body…it cannot be changed; same form. Even if they are older they won't look older…we can grow but same face.

What do you wear?

We wear clothes but of very fine unseen particles.

With whom do you stay?

Granny, she loves me. When I came to her, she was extremely sorry, so she is with me, on the fifth plane. (There seems to be some contradiction here. Unless she was talking of her paternal grandmother as one of the grandmothers is on the sixth plane).

Do you meet M uncle?

We meet often. He stays with grandpa on the fifth plane.

Is your world same or different from this world?

Same but different light

My darling, do you know when I will be coming to your world? I am fed up of life.

Don't ask this. I feel all is God's will. None can avoid destiny. Time is fixed, even the place.

Will you be there to receive me?

Of course I will be there.

Do you come when I pray? Your photo moves when I touch it.

You must concentrate. Don't doubt when I move.

Why don't you come when I sit for automatic writing? What should I do to develop power?

Your mind must be calm. Go on trying and you will succeed. When you are quite free and fresh you sit for writing, I will come definitely.

How is Ketu?

Alright

The First Séance: Saturday April 25, 1978

This séance took place in G High School and was headed by Mr Phiroze Kapadia, the father figure to most psychic mediums in Mumbai. The medium would go into a trance, move about, halting in front of the person for whom the message was meant to be delivered. Below are passages from Vira's diary:

> The medium came straight to me and said, "Your prayers are being heard here, you are doing well, keep it up child." Then she went to G (Vira's sister) and told her that "someone wants to talk to you". That was my Cherzi who on seeing G, broke down completely and had to be consoled by the rest of the mediums. Then she started talking to her ma. "Mummy, you have taught me the best qualities in life. To give, give and give." She said at times she used to get sore with her mother for teaching her the same old things but now she said that alone was helping her. Cherzi said her daddy's prayers were also helping her. Seeing G in the very same black dotted dress which she had worn on the day Cherzi boarded the ill-fated plane she said, "Mummy, why this dress again? You know I do not like mourning. Mourning is just to show the world, it's hypocrisy. You go out and see the beautiful world God has given you and the beautiful things around you."

> Then the guide through the medium went to Z and said, "You are God's good soul. You extend your loving arms to everyone." She was asked to look after G (Cherzi's mom) and giver her company. Then she said "You see light, you hear someone calling you when you are alone, but when you turn around there is nobody."

The Guide also went to B and said, "You called me your daughter; instead of my mummy," – it was to give us proof that Ketu had come. Then clinging to B she started crying.

"I love you" B in her turn became hysterical and answered back non-stop, "I love my baby, kill me first but I want my baby." She continued as if possessed. She had to be consoled by "prayers." The Guide got excited. "Shall I slap you now?" The meeting hence was very much disturbed. For Amy (Ketu's mother and the clairvoyant we have mentioned earlier), the Guide sent the following message through B. "Your sister prays the whole time and helps everyone around as and when she is needed and still she thinks to herself while she prays, "Oh God why, why....this shock and blow to me? Bring her to me. I want to explain to her. I want to console her," said the guide. (Amy refused to come).

The second séance could not be attended. The third séance was held on March 12, 1978. K, B and Vira attended it. G (Cherzi's mother) and Z could not make it.

The Guide went straight to K and said, "Now you have stopped fighting with me. Your sister has not come today but it does not matter, tell her not to argue with him. (Cherzi's dad). Being the father, he wants to show his authority. He will understand by and by." Then the Guide walked up to me (Vira) and said, "You will be able to tell your sister better. You will understand what I want her to do." Then she continued. "Tell her to take a prayer book and pray loudly and concentrate and create vibrations. Then we will connect with her in thoughts with us here." Again she went to K and asked her to thank Z (who had not attended that day). *"Thank your friend for the devotion she has shown you in your hour of need".*

Then she went to B and Ketu spoke through the medium. *"I love mummy. I miss mummy."* Again the Nun's Guide said that the children could not come without permission. Seeing the medium walk towards me, I requested the Guide to look after our children. She got a little annoyed and said, *"You don't have to tell us."* I began to cry hearing her say that our children were well cared for. She saw me crying and scolded me. *"Again you are crying! Shall I stop the meeting?"* I said sorry and assured her that I would not cry.

G had asked through Phiroze's Guide whether Cherzi and Ketu would have survived if they had not boarded the ill-fated plane. We wanted to tape the answer for G. Phoroze's Guide began to speak.

"The philosopher started laughing. Do you ever question when there is birth? Then why do you question thus at the time of death? No, he said, birth and death are given to you by the law. You cannot change it."

Fourth séance, held on Saturday, March 25, 1978

G, K and Z did not come. But Faranak, B and I had gone. That day our Medium, Arnavaz Kapadia (wife of Phoiroze Kapadia) was not keeping very well so she was hesitating to hold the meeting. Her daughter coaxed her, however, and the meeting was half. First the Guide went straight to Hufrish, Kapadia's daughter and said, "For your selfish motives you will have to be quick otherwise my power will wane." True enough, she used to fade often. Going to Faranak, Vira's daughter, she told her to "have more faith in prayers my child, as that alone will help you. Don't be ashamed of your beautiful mother. She is a high soul. Try to understand her and don't run her down".

To me she said: "First I must scold you. You think of the children too often and that will not help you reach God. Try to reach the Almighty through prayers and direct thought and not through your children. Your child is here and says – "Aunty, my father snubs you in very diplomatic ways by banging doors, banging tables etc but do not take notice; he will understand. How I wish to sit on your lap and hug you as I used to do." Then Cherzi confirmed my dream of March 12 saying she was testing me by saying she was being sent away for three months. She wanted to know whether I would still attend the séance.

There are a number of such communications but I have taken those which I felt, spoke more about the other world rather than personal conversations. (This diary I got six months later). Now back to my meeting with Vira.

"Who came into your life first? Meher Baba or Guru Nanak?

"Guru Nanak. Actually He began to communicate with us in 1981, but neither Cheherazade nor Guru Nanak revealed their identity. But the words that poured forth from this new visitor were so poetic, prolific and philosophical that I was certain that this Guide was the spirit of no ordinary mortal."

"Often I would ask this heavenly Guide for a name. I was certain that this Guide was a God incarnate. In fact, Meher Baba holds Him is in very high esteem. Everyday I would ask Guru Nanak to divulge His name and everyday He would say what difference does a name make? He would keep writing, what is in a name? Then once He told me the reason, why He was not divulging His name. He said that he wanted me to read His lectures delivered to me, ponder over them, think out the essence and only if I was certain that what was in the lectures was true, should I believe and follow his preaching. He did not want me to follow His words blindly. He said that if He divulged who He was then I would follow whatever He wrote without thinking.

One day He finally said that I could call Him whatever I wanted; Ram. Shyam anything. That day He ended His lecture by singing off as Ciam. Pronounced like Shyam."

"Then how did you find out?"

"Have you met Amy?"

"No."

"Amy too lost her daughter Ketu in the same flight which killed Cheherazade. Amy is a very powerful clairvoyant."

"Eh?" Inquired the one who was supposed to write a book on the paranormal world.

"She can see spirits, I can't. I can communicate with them whereas she can see them. One day when I sat down for auto-writing Amy arrived. Ciam was communicating with me at that time. After He signed off and I stood up to greet Amy, she smiled and told me that the mystery of who Ciam was had been solved. I was shocked. When she said Guru Nanak was Ciam, I was stunned. Why Guru Nanak? Just like Meher Baba, though I respected Guru Nanak I did not worship Him. Now I have realised that it does not matter what your religion is and who you worship. Your Guides do not discriminate as per religion. Also, Guides such as Meher Baba and Guru Nanak are not the sole property of anybody. They may be Guides to thousands of people. They function at different levels of consciousness."

The next day when Vira sat down for auto-writing, the first line from Ciam was that He was Guru Nanak. (In fact, fortunately I came across that very message in which Guru Nanak for the first time revealed His identity). But He insisted that He be called Ciam. He once again insisted that Vira should not follow His teachings blindly but only after adequate thought and contemplation.

No prophet wants His followers to blindly accept what is being preached. Zarathustra, the oldest known Prophet, who is believed to have lived around 1500 BC too had insisted that he wanted only those in His faith, who had given thought to what He preached. He wanted people to contemplate, rationalise and only then decide to follow the faith set out by Him, Zarathustra; the faith which preaches the philosophy that there is just one God, whichever name you call Him (Lord Ahura Mazda in Persian) and that the way to His heart was through Good Thoughts, Good Words and Good Deeds – the three pillars of Zoroastrianism. He wanted a thinking race. Thus even in 1500 BC and virtually at the fag end of the 21st century, two prophets insisted on a thinking race; amazing!

"If I want to know who my Guides are, can you find out?"

I will try. Sometimes it takes a lot of time for a Guide's name to be divulged. Many times the name may mean nothing to us but the Guide could yet be a much evolved soul. Like Pheroze's Guide who is a Buddhist or Chinese monk. We think He is a Lama. He is a very evolved soul but we had never heard of him. Earlier, I used to not only give the name of the Guide but through automatic writing, even draw the picture of other people's Guides.

"I have another way of finding out who your Guides are – sit in front of a diva and meditate. Or just mediate. Ask your Guides to show themselves to you. Sit every day for about half-an-hour and just meditate on this. I guarantee you that within a month's time you shall get the names of your guides and how they look; either during mediation or in your sleep."

"Do you still get messages through auto-writing or in your sleep?"

"Nowadays I get messages anytime. I rarely sit for auto-writing and even if I do, I have to write fast as thoughts flash through my mind and I have to race to copy them. Ciam goes at rapid speed. I get messages in the mind any time. I hear the voice in my head…"

"His voice…"

"I cannot explain, but yesterday as I was praying, Baba informed me that He had sent you to me for a specific purpose; that you were a genuine person. I am certain that it is Meher Baba speaking and not my subconscious mind; because yesterday I was deep in prayer and had nobody in my mind. After he spoke about you, He asked me to give my friend S… a call and tell her that she has a very bad case of diabetes and that she must take long walks every day without fail. He then insisted that I tell her that if she did not take regular walks and exercise, her legs would have to be amputated. Now a thought like this can never enter my mind. First of all I have not met S…. for a long time. We are friends but not very close. I felt so odd making the call but I knew I had to as Baba wanted me to make the call. Earlier I used to avoid informing people as I felt very embarrassed. But he used to get upset with me for doubting Him. So many times, people make fun of you and some feel you are encroaching on their privacy. It is a very odd situation for me to be in. but I rang up S…. First I apologised and then asked her how she was keeping. She was surprised naturally that out of nowhere Vira remembered her. So he told me that she was not keeping well. Then I cautiously asked her if she was suffering from diabetes? I could make out that she was shocked and asked how I knew of a problem which only her immediate family were aware of? I told her that Meher Baba had left a message for her and was she interested in hearing it? She seemed so taken aback that she mumbled that she herself was going to give me a call and request me to ask Meher Baba regarding her health. Then I told her what Baba had informed, that if she did not take regular walks and exercise, her legs would have to be amputated. I could make out over the phone that S… was stunned. Then in a soft voice she informed me that the same morning her own doctor had said the very same thing. When Baba was telling me about her amputation, S's doctor was giving her the same message; so you see, I receive messages. How could my mind think up such an accurate message for S…? Okay, as far as you are concerned maybe I liked you at first sight and my subconscious mind took over from there but what about S…?"

"How did Meher Baba enter you life?"

"I was going through a very bad phase in life. I had just lost my husband and I was having other personal problems. Of course, in those days I still did not believe in Meher Baba or for that matter any sort of fakir, sadhu etc. I was born in a priestly family. Staunch Zoroastrians who only worshipped our Lord Ahura Mazda, our prophet Zarathustra and visited only the fire-temple and prayed from the Avesta.

"I had heard of Meher Baba but never prayed to Him or even believed Him to be God incarnate. Many of my friends worshipped Meher Baba and Sai Baba of Shirdi but not me."

Many people in every religion have a condescending attitude towards other religions. Many are made to believe since childhood that their religion, their prophet, their God – known by different names – and their prayers constitute the true faith.

To such people, everyone else belonging to other religions is wasting their time and effort. Many truly believe that when they stop infesting the earth and haul their pious asses to the world beyond, because of their particular religion, they shall be given the red carpet treatment and handed a green card, proclaiming them as life members of the heavenly club.

"That day I was particularly sad. I sat for prayers and tears were flowing down my cheeks. I had shut my eyes and was beseeching God for help. Suddenly, though my eyes were shut, a light shone brightly in my head and I saw the vision of a very noble looking man. For a while I did not recognise who it was; then it struck me that He was Meher Baba. Though at first I did not recognise Him and later when I did, I still thought that my sadness was playing tricks with me. I mean why Meher Baba should be smiling at me when I really did not even believe in Him? He spoke to me and though I heard Him it was in my mind that I heard His voice. He said that he knew that I was going through a bad phase but now that He had arrived, my bad days had just ended. Then He said 'I have been asked to take care of you by your friend A'."

Vira's friend was an ardent follower of Meher Baba. She had died some time before this incident took place.

"Baba said to me, 'your friend scolded me by saying that if I could take care of the whole world's problems, why I was not doing anything for you? You who are her best friend? You know how insistent this friend of yours can get. So here I am. Do not worry. Leave everything in my hands. Every day, sit for prayers and remember me. I shall communicate with you every day. So every day I used to sit for meditation and He would communicate with me through the pen or through the planchette. My problems got solved. I also realised that Meher Baba was my guide, my guardian angel."

One thing is certain; Meher Baba loves humour and laughter.

Even while writing this book, everybody insisted that I try to make the book light reading as Meher Baba loved a good laugh.

I wondered aloud whether Vira ever doubted the vision in which Meher Baba had paid her the first visit.

"No. At first I still could not believe that Meher Baba had visited me but in my heart I knew He had, because I felt so nice and peaceful that I know only God could have made me feel so. I became His follower that very moment. Now I cannot think of life without Him. I do not know what will happen to me if he stops communicating and guiding me. Yes, earlier I used to wonder; of all the people why did he choose me? But now I no longer ask Him questions. He knows best."

It was through Meher Baba that Vira learnt another important fact.

"Meher Baba, through auto-writing, informed me that not only was He my guardian angel but that each person has not one, but many Guides. In fact, He informed me that each of us has a group of spirits, guides and angels whose main aim is to guide the person to the path of God with the final aim of making that person live only for God and then eventually to merge with Him. Guides change from time to time, depending upon a person's level of spiritual growth. It is like when a child is in the first standard, he has a particular group of teachers. When the child goes to the ninth standard the group of teachers is obviously different and when the child is doing his post-graduation degree, the professors will be different, more qualified and better equipped to impart such knowledge. So is the case with a person growing spiritually; the more spiritually advanced and inclined a person is the higher is the level of evolution of his guardian angel and guide."

According to Vira, Meher Baba then further elaborated that often a person becomes weak in mind and begins to indulge in vices and falls prey to evil. Automatically his guardian angels or guides change. From highly evolved spirits, the person gets less enlightened souls as his guides. Maybe, a few months or years later, the person once again wills himself to walk the path of righteousness and shuns evil and vice; automatically his Guides change and more evolved spirits once again take over.

Apart from Vira, a number of psychics have mentioned that each of us has Guides taking care of us and guiding us to get more spiritually inclined and thus, more spiritually evolved. Ruth Montgomery, the world-renowned author on paranormal activities mentions a similar spiritual working pattern. In fact, through auto-writing, her Guides have made her write a number of books on paranormal subjects.

"Frankly son, in the beginning I did not understand all this. I am an ordinary person. I have not done anything exceptional in life to become a medium. I was religious but never so much that I should be singled out by Meher Baba. When sometimes I inquire as to why a number of us have been singled out, Meher Baba mentions that we are not on earth for the first time. We have incarnated countless times and in all probability most shall come back a number of times. We come to earth with Karma (accountability of actions committed either in past lives or in the present; as you sow so shall you reap), and go back with a bag full of karmas. Maybe my karma in my past life or lives was very good. Maybe I had some relation with Meher Baba. I don't know and to tell you frankly I do not give all this much thought."

Now after knowing Vira and meeting her so many times, I do believe her. She is amazingly detached and casual about her powers. She is as amazed about her spiritual prowess as those who are close to her are impressed by her being a medium. Even she gets surprised when predictions she voices are so accurate.

"As I said earlier each one of us has a number of guides. I assume there is a main Guide or two main Guides. Usually a family member or a close friend becomes a Guide of someone he or she has known in this or other lives. Of course, the Guide too has to be highly evolved. Earlier, a number of souls used to communicate with me but since Meher Baba has entered my life, Cheherazade, Ketu, and all our family members come very rarely. They have informed us that they had to move on with other things and would come on rare occasions. Now only Meher Baba and Guru Nanak communicate with me through auto-writing and the planchette."

The phone rang again. After a while Vira stood up and informed that she had to meet a friend in a few minutes.

I nodded and stood up to leave. It was very late. Spiritual talks interest me a lot. I can forget everything at such times but an abnormally upset wife at home, waiting to go for a drive with terrorist-like kids can rouse me out of any sort of stupor. I thanked Vira for her time.

"Meher Baba has asked me to invite you to attend our meetings. We have a small gathering every alternate Wednesday. Meet me here at five-thirty this coming Wednesday. We start at six. Not many people, just 10 to 12. But please don't tell anybody or get anybody. I would not like people to know about this."

I nodded and sighed. At last I was going to sit in a séance.

Having finished re-reading *Autobiography of a Yogi*, I wanted to read literature, which complimented what I had read from the great book. A number of doubts persisted and I needed some confirmation from other sources, distinctly different from Eastern Sages. So I picked up a number of books by Ruth Montgomery, the world renowned author of innumerable books on life after death and other paranormal happenings and was pleasantly surprised that she too believed in the same theory which appears in Sri Paramhansa Yogananda's *Autobiography of a Yogi* and divulged by Sri Paramhansa Yogananda's guru, Sri Sri Swami Sri Yuketeswar Giri.

Ruth Montgomery has written numerous books, but she has repeatedly confessed that she acts only as a medium for her Guides to type out their wisdom. "Readers of my previous books on psychic subjects are aware that after meditating each morning, I rest my fingers lightly on the typewriter keys, while still in that so-called alpha state and with eyes closed, transmit what the Guides wish to type during the 15-minute period."

The concept that there are many planets and many worlds exist and that each is meant for inhabitants who have reached a particular spiritual level is known to all mystics and most psychics. It is also well known that the earth is certainly not the only planet which sustains life and where civilisations exist.

"The Guides told me long ago that we human souls all began simultaneously as 'sparks of God'. The souls in other galaxies are just as much a part of the Creator as we are. They originated as did we, in that original burst of creative energy in which all souls began as companions and co-creators with God. When some of them felt attracted to certain planets and galaxies, they went there as pioneers to help subdue and regulate the elements and the beasts of the field and because there proved to be great harmony between them and the sometimes difficult terrain and atmospheric conditions, they remained there for longer and longer periods to turn those stumbling blocks into stepping stones."

"It is somewhat different with our own planet earth, which came into existence later. Here, souls first entered the bodies of animals and birds and fish (sic) and because of this tampering with God's act of creation, earthlings fell from grace for a long period of time, until a prototype was created as Adam, with Eve as his mate. God-like souls cohabited with those who had previously entered animals' bodies. Intercourse with animals, fish and fowl produced large, misshapen offspring, some of whom were nevertheless so talented that they later came to be worshipped in Greek and Roman mythology. These are simply names for the first man and woman to inhabit what we term a human body and those who come here from other planets are able to create a duplicate of this body that is so well suited to the earth's atmosphere and the need to walk about."

"Thus, although body types differ on other planets, this is found to be the most satisfactory one for the earth and in the early days these bodies were kept healthy and functioning for many hundreds of years. The so-called space people are in actuality like us. We are also space people in the sense that all of us live in a universe that is whirling in orbit. When these souls who inhabit other spheres visit the earth, they come as humanoids… to understand why they arrive on earth is to explore the plan of universal brotherhood, since all of us began as sparks cast off by the Creator. As these souls acquired identities and free will, they moved from one space to another and some of them shone brilliantly as true companions of the Creator, while others developed delusions of grandeur as co-creators and sought to impose their will on others. Some visited the earth, while others sought experience on different planets and orbs. They are no more alien than you or we are, except that the earth is not their original planet."

"Those who visit the earth at this time are from planets with highly advanced technology and science. They have solved the challenge of space travel through dissolving atoms and reconstituting them in the earth's atmosphere and on other planets. Space aliens are able to dissolve the atomic structures of their spaceships as well as their bodies and to reassemble the atoms as they reach the earth's outer stratosphere. It is a feat that some earthlings with extraordinary psychic talents have also been able to perform within the earth's atmosphere. We speak now of the Avatars (God Incarnates) and certain Hindu Yogis in particular. Usually such enlightened people have recalled the memory of how to perform that feat from previous lifetimes on other planets that are more advanced scientifically as well as spiritually than the earth. Bear in mind that the two are not necessarily synonymous. To be technically advanced is not necessarily being spiritually advanced."

"On some planets the inhabitants are so close to the Creator that they commune easily with His (God's) spirit plane, while on others they are so far advanced technologically that they can dissolve atoms, relocate them by mental powers alone and reassemble them wherever they wish, yet have lost the ability to commune directly with the Godhead. There are some planets which combine the best qualities of both and a few that unfortunately combine the worst of both worlds."

At first when I read Ruth Montgomery's *Aliens Amongst Us*, I read it (parts of it as I am not much of a space man) with a large dose of scepticism. But ironically, it was the last chapter, the afterword, in *Aliens Amongst Us* that got me thinking. I quote an extract from Ruth Montgomery's book:

"The Old Testament account by Prophet Ezekiel of his encounter with four space aliens, who took him in a UFO from Babylon to Jerusalem, is a case in point. In the sixth century BC, the Jewish race was in grave danger of extinction through absorption. King Nebuchadnezzar had besieged Jerusalem three times, taking captive 10,000 craftsmen, artisans, brave warriors and princes, including Ezekiel and also carrying off to Babylon all of the treasures and golden vessels from King Solomon's Temple. Only the poorest of the poor were left in Palestine and the absent Ezekiel worried about those leaderless Jews who were forsaking the one God and intermarrying with soldiers of the occupational army."

"Ezekiel had been a captive in Babylon for more than 30 years when one day, while sitting by the river Chebar, he beheld a UFO approaching from the north and landing by his side. The Book of Ezekiel gives a graphic description of the flying saucer and of the four men who emerged from it and tells of his trial run that day in the flying machine. Although nearly scared out of his wits, he bravely visited the spot a week later and again saw the UFO with its occupants. On his third encounter he actually flew with them to Jerusalem, where he visited the devastated city and the desecrated temple for several days, talking to the Jews, before the spaceship returned and flew him back to Babylon.

"Another example is given by Brad Lemley who states that in the fifteenth century BC, King Thutmose III of the Egyptian Eighteenth Dynasty saw 'a circle of fire coming in the sky...one rod long was its body and a rod wide and it was noiseless,' and the sky was later filled with many such circles (or flying saucers). In 329 BC, two shining silver shields dived repeatedly at the army of Alexander the Great and in Germany in 1561 'the sky was filled with cylindrical shapes from which emerged black, red, orange and blue-white spheres that darted about', a good description of a mother ship releasing her cargo of flying saucers. And all of these occurrences remember, were in the days when nothing was supposed to be flitting about in our skies except birds."

But of greatest interest in *Aliens Among Us*, was the reference to Babaji. Who is Babaji? In the *Autobiography of a Yogi*, Babaji's reference is made with awe and reverence. The book is written by Sri Paramhansa Yogananda. His guru is the enlightened Sri Sri Swami Yuketswar Giri, who resurrected and divulged to his disciple, the truths of different worlds and the stages of evolution of the soul till it is ready to merge with God. The guru of Sri Sri Swami Yuketswar Giri is the well loved, Sri Sri Lahiri Mahasaya, the supreme one. Now Babaji is the guru of Sri Sri Lahiri Mahasaya. Babaji is known as the Deathless Guru.

According to Sri Sri Lahiri Mahasaya, "Babaji has been chosen by God to remain in his body for the duration of this particular world cycle. Ages will come and go – still the deathless master, beholding the drama of the centuries shall be present on this stage terrestrial."

Ruth Montgomery writes: "In India, Babaji is called Mahavatar, *The Great Incarnation* and his presence was first revealed to the Western world in 1946 through Paramhansa Yogananda's *Autobiography of a Yogi*, which described him as the 'the deathless avatara' and declared that 'the secluded Master has retained his physical form for centuries, perhaps for millennia' in order to uplift humanity."

"John (an alien in a human body) says of Babaji: 'One day in a flash, it was given that without the presence of Babaji and his spiritual family on the planet, many souls of high spiritual standing would not be able to incarnate here from other planetary systems without tremendous struggle to maintain spiritual balance because of the intense discord on planet earth. This Master (Babaji) is fully merged with God and is known as the Supreme Servant. His presence creates a tremendous spiritual polarisation that establishes a strong field of righteousness and harmony about the earth plane. This polarisation creates a tremendous spiritual attraction for all good souls to come here. Thus, by Babaji's mere presence on this planet, many other great souls and lovers of God are enabled to come here, for I assure you that were it not for the presence of Babaji, none of us would be able to stand the intense discord of this plane. Babaji promised that he would not leave his physical body until the end of this particular world cycle and we should all be grateful for the tremendous sacrifice that he has undertaken for the children of the earth. Babaji is indeed in flesh whenever He chooses to exercise His right to a body that continues to flourish in India. He is a source of wonderment for those who are privileged to meet Him. Space people are aware of His existence and are drawn to Him as moths to a flame, but there would be some dissension if they all flocked to India and not to the Western world where the leadership currently rests and the need is greatest for benevolence and understanding of all peoples....'

"Continue Ruth's Guides: 'Yogananda is an avatara who now freely comes and goes as He pleases and is sometimes with Babaji in the Himalayas. The latter's physical body is kept alive through fresh air, sunlight and spiritual repast, for He seldom eats other than the occasional nectar and water. These completed ones who have worked off all karma, need not replenish themselves with earthly food unless they so choose.'"

I read all these portions amazed. If doubts ever existed in my mind, they were erased. But truly, I am not surprised at God's diverse range of capabilities. From Babaji, the deathless guru to Bharucha, The Confused One, everything is possible in life.

Not just on the physical plane but till we all meet and become one with God.

Wednesday came after years. Seconds dragged and I was accused of being impatient. At last I parked the bike and strode up the stairs leading to Vira's flat. The door was opened by another lady. Though she smiled and looked at me, I noticed and felt that she had looked at me, within me and through me.

"Ruzbeh?"

"Ahhh yes!"

"I am Amy"

Amy was Ketu's mother. Ketu and Cheherazade had expired together in the ill-fated air crash. I also recollected that Amy was a clairvoyant who had revealed the identity of Guru Nanak. I entered and shut the door behind me. I wanted desperately to inquire if any aggrieved spirit hovered around me. I was all for spirits to hover around me. Especially noble, pure hearted, spiritually evolved, financially sound and benevolent spirits were always welcome. But I have been often told; more so by family members, that no normal person would behave the way I do, going about sleepwalking through life. So I was curious to know whether a spirit with a devious sense of humour, bordering on the slapstick, operated behind this noble-minded author.

Amy left the room to call Vira and I sat on my usual reclining chair in the balcony. Though it was five, the sun glared at me from a cloudless sky. I felt it had no right to get so particular about making life so sticky, blazing and….my eyes nearly dashed out of my socket. A couple, may be just in love, sat on a bench, bang in the sun, no shade, looking into each other's eyes. I looked at them aghast. What made rational-minded folk behave like deranged mules? I pondered. Cupid must be one demented spirit I concluded. Constantly in demand, the poor blighter had snapped important wire connections making people do insane things when in love.

Vira approached and I once again realised that I was fortunate to have been directed to this remarkable woman. She exuded certain maternal warmth, which made you feel that God was not only content to be in heaven but to spend lots of time on planet earth.

"How are you dear boy?"

"Very keen to attend the first séance."

"I have an important message to deliver to you. Meher Baba has told me a lot about you. According to Him you are a good soul but it is time you got stable in your life. He also says that you have gone through a hard life and yet a lot of hardship is ahead. But you will see it through. He wants you to know that He is there to protect you through your ordeals and put you on safe shores. But get some stability in your life. It is a must. Another important thing I inquired was about the identity of your guides. He has given me two names. Your main Guide, your principal Guardian Angel, is Sai Baba of Shirdi. Your other important Guide is Dastoorji Narihoshang Dhaval, who is another powerful soul. He is one of the most revered priests whose name also comes in our prayers. Sai Baba of Shirdi you of course know." I found it hard to speak.

"I am a devout follower of Sai Baba of Shirdi."

The phone disrupted our conversation. It was a call from USA and Vira commenced to speak to the person at the other end of the line. I wondered, if two persons could converse with each other, both sitting at two different ends of the globe, why people found it so hard to believe that spirits could communicate with mankind through just a veil that separates the two dimensions?

Not finding an answer immediately, my thoughts went back to my Sai Baba.

Since I can remember, Sai Baba has been a part of my life consciously or otherwise. My maternal grandmother, as I have already mentioned earlier, worships Sai Baba with immense faith and love. Any calamity or occasion of happiness, Sai Baba is an integral part of the proceedings. I first went to Shirdi with my grandmother. We cousins, who are as close as siblings from the same womb, my grandmother, my eldest aunt, Nargish Bengali who has taken care of us kids like a mother; we all went to bow our heads, open our hearts, fold our hands and pay obeisance to Sai Baba. Ironically, I do not remember much about my childhood, though I do remember the pilgrimage to Shirdi vividly.

Then virtually a decade and more elapsed till a few years ago I was slowly drifting away from God. Moving towards the tawdry, shallow world where priorities began to be measured with the jingle of money. Of course, before wife, family and moralists begin to roll up their sleeves; I would like to make a point clear. I was not becoming corrupt, debased, devoid of morals and all that jazz. I was simply experiencing a shift in priorities, placing Gold before God. A subconscious shift covered by placing the blame on priorities. Like a badly written script…*I did all this for you and now you ask me from where I got the money to pay for your Merc?* I was becoming a stranger to myself and soul, a stranger lost in the hustle of life. Losing touch with the soul is as bad as becoming corrupt or debased. All religions begin and end with the self; for it is the self, each single soul, which is a part of God and God is thus a part of each single self.

The trend of events began when one day a friend gave me a pen with Sai Baba's photograph on the cap. A few days later my parents gave me a huge calendar with a beautiful photograph of Baba as well as High blessings to His devotees printed under the photograph. A week later another friend gave me prasad (holy offerings of sweet-meat or other preparations, kept during prayers or offered first to God and then distributed to devotees), from Sai Baba's temple at Shirdi. I understood that Sai Baba was calling me to His *samadhi,* the final resting place of the Master.

I wanted to go to Shirdi, I did. It was a journey filled with miracles.

I reached Mumbai and life moved on. I had promised that every Thursday I would abstain from eating non-vegetarian food. Two Thursdays galloped by and on the third Thursday, after a rather tiring day at work (I was at that time, the Executive Editor of the fastest growing magazine in a well-known publishing house), I prepared a whisky and soda for myself. I was about to take a sip when my wife stood before me and stared hard.

"What?"

"That is exactly what I want to ask you. What are you doing?"

"Is this a case of partial amnesia or does this style of questioning have a purpose?"

"Today is a Thursday…."

"Very good and what shall tomorrow be young goat…?"

"Ruzbeh, today is a Thursday and you are drinking liquor. Today is Sai Baba's day. Have you already forgotten?"

"No, I haven't forgotten. But what has liquor got to do with either a Thursday or Sai Baba? I don't remember including liquor in my abstaining list. It was just no non-vegetarian sweetheart."

She shrugged her shoulders and made a face which left no doubt in any body's mind that she did not approve of what I was about to do.

"I still think you should not drink today. Anyway, it's between you and Sai Baba."

I took a small sip. Why can't man make a pact with God without ifs and buts? I went to take another sip and the glass flew from my hand and banged against the adjacent wall. The whisky splashed all over the wall and the glass split into small fragments all over the floor.

The glass had not slipped out of my hand. It had been thrown on the wall, a few feet away. It was as though an invisible force had hit my hand and the force had made the glass fly to the wall and then break into small fragments.

The force with which the glass had flown out of my hand left little to doubt. Sai Baba had taken the issue of my drinking on Thursdays in His hands.

It has been years since I drank liquor on Thursdays. I have also stopped smoking as well as eating non-veg on His day.

Vira put the phone down.

"Ruzbeh, come let us go for the séance."

We walked for a few minutes and knocked at a ground floor door. It belonged to Frenny, a woman who has spent a lifetime in séances and is a store house of knowledge on the occult and the paranormal world. The meeting took place every alternate Wednesday at 6 pm at Frenny's residence. She is an amazing woman. (As weeks would go by, I would get to know Frenny better and my respect for her would grow.)

She is virtually blind, big built, and has numerous physical ailments that often make her bedridden. She still lives all alone and manages her life admirably well.

"My guru, Satya Narayanji takes care of me."

I was introduced to the group. Amongst them was former Miss India, Meher Castillino, to whom I shall be forever indebted. She has generously lent me her expensive books on paranormal literature and I can say for certain that my horizon on this subject has broadened due to Meher's unstinted support.

"Ruzbeh, do your kusti prayers in the prayer room." We Zoroastrians wear a muslin vest and tie a fine intricately made thread around our waists. We tie it reciting our Mazdayasni prayers. The reason for tying the kusti, according to me is two-fold. First of all, after bath every morning when you have to wear the sudra and kusti you remember God and thus pray. If the sudra and kusti were not present, I wonder how many of us would even spend the three to five minutes in prayer. The second reason I deduced from reading Ruth Montgomery's book called *The Greatest Healer of Our Time* was that every planet has a magnetic ring around it which protects the planet from whirling off into the cosmos and colliding with other galaxies. Similarly, the kusti acts as a magnetic ring, which prevents the user, if tied with the right prayers and devotion, from hurtling off into negative and evil attitudes and being protected from negative and evil influences. This is my logic. I do not want Zoroastrian priests and moralists baying for my blood. Take it or leave it.

I said my prayers in the room. There were photographs of different God Incarnates: Avatar Meher Baba, Sai Baba, Zarathustra, Swami Narayan, Kamu Baba and many other Masters. The group assembled. The core group sat around a large table, while a few of us sat behind them due to want of space. The room was well lit, the sunbeams entered and played upon us, throwing vague shadows on the wall. The planchette was in front of Vira, while Amy sat by her side.

The séance began. I breathed in deep and we began to pray first our short Avesta prayers (Yatha Ahu Vairyo and Ashem Vahu) and then loudly chanted the word OM, the magical word that cleanses the soul as well as the surroundings of all negativity and paves the way for evolved spirits to make their presence felt. Then the planchette began to move. It wrote, I am Meher Baba....

After the séance, all the way back home I was extremely depressed. I poured myself a stiff whisky and added just a splash of soda. I sat in the bedroom and gazed at the diva and Meher Baba in particular. He grinned at me. I groaned and looked away.

"What's the matter with you? You're behaving as though a spirit punched you on the nose."

Not just any footloose spirit but God incarnate.

"The last time you were so depressed was when you had, due to dire financial constrains, changed your cigarette brand from Kent to Four Square."

I sighed. Often women have humour of a badly made Hindi horror movie. I took another gulp of whisky and grimaced. Boy, this was melted gun powder bottled as liquor to wipe out unsuspecting mankind.

"If you crack a joke about spirit communication or my occult gang or the book I am supposed to be writing, I shall speak to you when the kids graduate. And going by their track record it shall take decades. I...uh..I was told in the séance by Meher Baba that I was treating this whole séance business as a joke, as a game. But dash it, I have never been more serious in my life. Only the metaphysical world makes sense to me. I am very serious about all this stuff. "

"But why are you so depressed? Meher Baba said the truth. You treat everything as a game…."

"Whose side are you on, drinking my whisky, standing on my toe and gibbering nonsense? I do not treat this as a game or a joke…."

"My dear unemployed editor, you don't seem to realize that you treat the whole world, your work, your life, everything as a joke, as a Game. Our biggest problems have arisen because of your tendency to treat life as a joke. If you can treat life as a game, a joke, then why can't you treat death as a joke too?"

I shut my eyes and took another gulp of fire.

"Did Meher Baba say you don't believe in all this dhatum-dhitum (Not a very polite way of describing the paranormal world and its goings-on). Even He knows you believe in all this. It's just that you aren't serious about anything. So why would you get serious about death and what goes on after we all die? He is right; you must be treating all this as a joke and that is why He told you to get a little serious. Now are you coming to have dinner or are you going to kill yourself drinking this kerosene?"

After food, after Pashaan and Vahishta had once again tired everybody and themselves too, the Bharucha family, which consisted of my dad, mom, myself, wife, two barbarians (read as children), a maid, a temperamental dog and a detached tortoise, slept. Well except me. I woke up and lit a cigarette in the drawing hall and leafed through the book Frenny had lent me. *We Don't Die…George Anderson's Conversations With The Other Side* by Joel Martin and Patric Romanowski. I began to read it at 11, Wednesday and finished the book by two in the afternoon Thursday. I read it at two sittings. The first one lasted for a few hours and the next for just two; a fantastic book, well written.

One of the important differences between George Anderson and other psychic mediums is that George's openness has been tested under different and difficult situations. He has been put under test by so many sceptics that it would be difficult to jot down all those experiments in this book. The most interesting of the investigations is the one conducted by the co-author of the book, Joel Martin, a radio and television host and producer, who had publicly exposed frauds and was known for his thorough research. He met George Anderson in 1980. A colleague of Joel was insistent that he meet George Anderson, then an unknown psychic, who was remarkably accurate. In the end, Joel had no choice but to relent. The persistent colleague, needless to say, was a woman, Madeline.

One day George was brought to the studio and introduced to Joel. The meeting and the subsequent experiment are described hereafter.

"Madeline tells me that you receive messages from the dead," I (Joel) said.

"From those on the other side," he answered, almost apologising for correcting me.

"Do you know how or when it's happening?"

"No"

"Don't they call people like you a medium?"

"Well some people do. Actually I think I'm more small (size) than a medium," he quipped smiling.

Though Joel Martin had years of experience (not all very pleasant) with those involved with para-psychology, he still felt curious to know this shy, humble, unpretentious man. With George's permission, Joel commenced to take a test of the former's skills of being a medium.

George then said that he was ready to start. He had asked for several blank sheets of paper and a pen. These, he explained, were for the automatic writing. He warned me to answer his questions only by indicating 'yes' or 'no' and not to offer any information beyond that: "Let the spirits do the work." He prayed, ('Let the Lord bless and keep me. May He show His face to shine upon me and give me peace and accuracy), crossed himself and began.

George looked at me and began writing rapidly. From where I sat I could not easily make out what he was writing. Before I could inquire, he asked, "Do you take the name Solomon?"

"Solomon," I returned rhetorically, neither affirming nor denying.

"Yes Solomon," George answered.

"Do you mean Sol?" I deliberately offered another version of the name as a test for George, knowing that in the majority of cases, the supposed psychic will pick up on the subject's 'clarification' and follow it. What I would try to find out was how firmly George held to his interpretation of the reading and how confident he was in his 'source'.

"No, actually, he's saying 'Solomon' to me."

"Yes, yes, I do."

"Father vibration," George continued.

"What does that mean, George?"

"It's father figure to you," he replied.

"No" Again, though I could guess that we were talking about my grandfather Solomon, a learned man and devout Orthodox Jew, I tried to throw George off his track by denying him.

"You're saying no. He's saying yes," George insisted.

"You hear him?"

"Yes"

"A father figure?" George repeated.

"Yes" After a brief pause, during which George continued his writing, he looked up and said, "Wait, I hear him clearer now. It's definitely a father figure. But he's saying 'grandfather,' Solomon was your grandfather?"

"Yes," I answered in surprise, amazed that George wasn't really asking me a question but asking me to confirm the information he was receiving from the other side.

"There's a Jewish star – you know, the Star of David – over your head."

Before I could think, I glanced up but of course saw nothing. I could see him drawing the star over and over. I meant to nod in the affirmative, but all I could do was shake my head in disbelief. Without my confirmation, George continued. "The Star of David; was your grandfather Solomon a very traditional Jew? Because that's what he's saying, he's saying he was a traditional

Jew."

"Yes," I answered.

"Your grandfather Solomon is saying he was very proud of you when you were confirmed. That was the high point for him, so to speak, where you were confirmed. But after your confirmation, things changed. Your grandfather says you left the faith, so to speak. At the time, that was a disappointment to him."

I nodded yes, for everything George was saying was true.

"There's a young woman with short blond hair standing behind you."

I spun around in my chair and again saw nothing.

"I see her spirit!" George exclaimed.

"You do?"

"Yes. She's saying you know who she is."

"Yes," I acknowledged.

"She passed suddenly."

"Yes"

"She's pointing to her head and face."

"Why?"

"She's trying to show me where she was hurt or injured. Was she killed quickly or instantly?"

"Yes."

"I can feel the pain in my head and face," George explained.

"She says it was an accident. It was an accidental form of passing. "

"Yes"

"Do you take the name Shirley?"

"Yes"

"That's her. She says you need to be stricter with your

daughter. She's moving her hand very quickly. Pointing her finger and waving it at you very quickly..."

"Stop!" I shouted, before realizing what I'd said and apologized. George ceased writing. I would not let him go further. This stranger had pried far enough into my personal life... looking down I could see that my knuckles had gone white from clutching the edge of the table.

George had been right about everything. The woman who came through was my late former wife Shirley, the mother of my daughter. She had been killed instantly just a year before when a car struck her as she crossed a Brooklyn street. George's physical description of her was accurate, as were the details of the location and type of injuries she sustained.

But the most astounding revelation was the hand gesture he described. Whenever Shirley became annoyed with me, she would rapidly move her hand, pointing her finger at me. Even the message George gave me regarding our daughter was exactly what Shirley would have said; she was much stricter with our daughter than I was. There were things only I knew, things I'd shared with no one.

Joel had discussed these intimate family matters with nobody. Also how could George have possibly known such intimate characteristics of Shirley like her habit of shaking her hand and pointing her finger, when excited; a characteristic shown only towards her husband, Joel Martin? This point, according to Joel Martin has never ceased to astound and astonish him.

Though sufficiently impressed, Joel Martin still desired more proof of George Anderson's authenticity. Consequently, Joel decided to once again test George but this time without the latter seeing the person being conversed with and talked about. He decided to test George through the telephone.

Joel contacted his internationally renowned para-psychologist friend, Stephen Kaplan and informed him of George Anderson, a psychic medium who had impressed him.

Joel wanted to investigate George further and Stephen was the perfect candidate. Being a para-psychologist and a teacher, Stephen "took pleasure in publicly exposing hoaxes and though Kaplan enjoys international reputation as a para-psychologist, he approaches the subject with more scepticism than just about anyone I've (Joel Martine) met."

At first George seemed reluctant and taken aback when asked to be investigated over the telephone. After much persuasion, the shy man gave in and agreed to be put under the microscope of scepticism.

Joel had not informed George about either the identity of the caller or a single detail of Kaplan or even from where the call would come. Below is how the conversation took place on that fateful day.

"Hello caller"

"Hello" Kaplan responded.

"George can hear you," I said. "Please don't say anything about yourself. And do not give your name. This is a closed-circuit demonstration of his skills. Just say 'hello' so George can hear your voice quality."

"I understand, "Kaplan replied. "Hello George."

Suddenly George looked very intense as he began writing rapidly across a sheet of paper. "I know this may sound strange," he began, "but someone asks me to ask you this. Are you a mature man?"

"Yes"

"Is there a woman close to you that has passed on?"

"Depends on what you mean?"

"She says you're over 30."

"Yes"

"Was there a woman in your household who had a great influence?"

"I had an aunt who passed on."

"Was she in your household a great deal when you were growing up?"

"Yes"

"Is this on your mother's side?"

"Oh yes."

"Was your aunt married?"

"Yes"

"Has her husband passed on also?"

"Yes"

"Okay, I feel him around also. Your aunt is around you because of great movement."

"I'm always in a state of flux," Kaplan replied.

"Do you take the name Elizabeth, living or deceased?"

"Yes, I know a woman who calls herself Elizabeth."

"She's not family. Are you in contact with her? Or were you recently?"

"Recently"

"Is there a business connection?"

"She's a client."

"Is she very emotional?"

"Yes"

"Does she have suicidal tendencies?"

"It wouldn't surprise me."

"If she contacts you, please give her time. She needs someone to talk to."

"Okay"

"Is there an illness in your family?"

"Yes"

"A male?"

"Yes"

"Is it physical or mental?" Kaplan asked.

"Physical, I'll say," George answered. *"Yes there is a physical illness, acondition in the chest?"*

"Absolutely"

"Would your aunt who passed on know this man also?"

"Oh yes."

"Is there a possibility – I 'm not predicting death...but is there a possibility that he could pass on?"

"Absolutely"

"Because the aunt is waiting for him; is he your brother?"

"No"

"Is he close like that?"

"The person who is ill...yes."

"Okay, because the brother vibration is very strong. Does this person who is ill have a blood relation close to you?"

"Absolutely"

"That's what it is, very close."

"Yes"

"Is this someone you've shared many experiences with?"

"All the time"

"That's where I'm getting the brother. It's someone who is very close. Is this person very, very weak?"

"Physically, yes."

"Are you on good terms with this person?"

"Yes"

"That's the thing. There are very close ties here. Has your father passed on?"

"Oh yes."

"Would your father know this person?"

"Absolutely"

"Yeah, that's the thing. Now I'm getting that it's a father-

son vibration."

"It certainly is."

"That's what he says. 'It's my son.' "

I interrupted. "Why don't you tell George who he's talking about, caller?"

Kaplan replied, "George is talking about me!"

I confirmed what Kaplan said. "That's right, George. You're talking about the caller?"

"This gentleman is the one who is very seriously ill?" George asked in total   surprise.

"Yes," Kaplan acknowledged.

George was stunned. He waited for a moment and then returned to the reading.

"Your father is very much around you. Was he a harsh man?"

"Yes"

"Do you take the name Jack?"

"Yes"

"Was he close to you?"

"He was my uncle. He was married to the aunt who I told you about before, who lived next door to us when I was growing up."

"Do you take the name Harry?"

"Harry was my grandfather."

"He's passed on also."

"Oh yes"

"Do you recall him very well?"

"Sure"

"Well, I don't know if I should tell you this. He's waiting for you also. They're around you because they're aware of your condition," George explained.

Kaplan quipped, "Tell them they can wait. I'm travelling soon – but physically, not astrally."

The reading concluded and George had been absolutely on the dot not only about Kaplan's family who had passed on to the other dimension but also regarding Kaplan's rapidly declining health and his soon approaching death. Kaplan had a severe heart problem diagnosed as arteriosclerosis. When Kaplan was asked about his views on George, the former replied that he felt George was genuine.

Another important insight into the working of George Anderson is that throughout the book he insists that he does not know where his powers come from. He has had this power ever since he can remember.

George Anderson contracted chicken fever when a child of six. The virus pounded his nervous system leading to inflammation of the brain and spinal cord which resulted in virtual paralysis. He could not even lift his head to drink water held to his lips. It took weeks before he partially recovered but he could not walk. He had to be carried from place to place. Then two months later, one morning George woke up, got out of bed and walked. Not only that, he was so overcome with joy that he ran all over the house. According to George it was after he had recovered from this illness that he began to hear voices and communicate with the dead. He then began to reveal intimate details of what had occurred to people in the past, referring to incidents that had taken place much before his birth as well as predicting the future. What relation the illness has with psychic ability is not clear to even George himself.

George Anderson does not rationalise his prowess. He lays great emphasis on the power of prayers and being positive. He also insists that often anger remains even after one's soul has left the physical body, till the soul realises that it is no more in the physical plane. Realisation and acceptance that you no longer are in the physical plane are of prime importance. A number of psychics have repeated over and over again that till the soul does not accept the fact that it has crossed over in reality, that what it experiences is not a dream, that it has to move on with life, that life exists after death, till then the soul remains neither in the spirit world nor in the physical plane. These souls are known as earthbound souls; drifting, may be for decades and more till they accept facts and move on with life. This is why it is of utmost importance that while living, the person acquires through religious books, books of the spirit world, knowledge and acceptance that after death too life goes on. We do not die. The soul is immortal. There is life in the next dimension. We are not our body. We are our soul; our vault of thoughts, experiences and karma.

It is a fascinating book, this '*We Don't Die........George Anderson's Conversations With The Other Side.*' It is a must read. It comforts one to know that your loved ones who have passed over await you. It comforts to know that you shall meet the old gang. It comforts to know that in the end so much depends on the individual person....not only on this plane but even above. When will such literature be made part of the educational curriculum, one wonders?

Life was getting nastier, a few family members behaving like strangers, work prospects seemed bleak and I barely had money to go through the following day and the month had just begun. Why is it that the moment you are in a financial crunch, expenses arrive in truckloads? I assume it is a universal phenomenon. I abhor such phenomena. Once again I sat for the séance. I sat far away from the group, head bent low, feeling extremely low when the planchette wrote:

"My child outside the circle." Then the planchette jumped from the board and moved towards me and halted in front of Frenny sitting in front of me. I stood up and touched the planchette in obeisance. "Don't let worries hamper your daily routine. All will be taken care of. You have been called here, so rest." I was moved to tears. No one knew I was going through a horrid phase. None knew I had disrupted my routine of prayers, writing and trying my best to live in the present; trying hard not to let bitter thoughts enter my head. Yes, my daily routine lay in tatters at the feet of my anger. Meher Baba had taken time off for me. I felt warm and wanted. In fact, I had beseeched Him to send me a message of comfort and He had obliged. I do not know whether anybody believes me or not. But for those who do believe, I can only say that God and His merry band of incarnates are aware of every thought, action, word and emotion. If you beseech God and whosoever you worship, They listen. Believe me friend, They do listen. And if you keep your mind calm, answers come. Assume your mind to be a slate or a sheet of paper. Keep the slate or paper clean (no thoughts, no emotions, no worry) and you will be surprised that the answers to your problems will in a short while be written in capital letters on the clean slate. You might get the solution in a flash, like an inspiration or through somebody or something, or even in your dreams. But for the answer to be written, the mind has to be clean. If your mind, the slate or the paper, is crowded with thoughts, emotions and worry, where is the space for Them to write to you? I know it may sound too simple but believe me: God is simple. Everything else is complex. A quote I have borrowed from Sri Paramhansa Yogananda's *Autobiography Of A Yogi*.

"A few lectures from Guru Nanak: One on how to pray and one on the Karmic link with those around us." Vira smiled and handed me the auto-written lectures.

In the short time I have spent reading books on the paranormal world as well as speaking to psychics, I have learnt that prayers matter a lot to those who have passed over. Sai Baba of Shirdi, Meher Baba and Guru Nanak have repeatedly insisted that the power of prayers works wonders and can really move mountains, not only for us folks still on the physical plane but even for those in the spirit world. Holy books have mentioned this fact, mediums are convinced that prayers help troubled souls going through troubled times (caused by their ignorance or being adamant not to accept the fact that they are no longer on the physical plane and that life does exist in the spirit world, or due to their deeds or unwillingness to leave the physical plane). Prayers help them to progress spiritually, which means prayers help the soul to move forward in the spiritual world.

According to George Anderson: "Prayers said for the departed, ceremonies performed after death, everyday prayers that are meant for the peace of the soul, really help and do wonders for our departed family and friends. I have had so many spirits telling me to thank their loved ones for praying for their souls. Prayers do wonders not only for us who are living but also for those living in the spirit world. I highly recommend that people pray for those who have passed on. It says so in scriptures and it is a good idea spiritually, especially for those who've had a traumatic passing or a suicide. You're embracing them with constant love and warmth, as you would here. You're sending them very positive energy that's helping them to find themselves and progress on the other side."

In George Anderson's book, John Lennon mentions to the former that the outburst of prayer for his well-being and the progress in the spirit world, by his millions of fans automatically made him progress to a higher phase.

One thing is certain: all souls do not assemble at one place. The concept of heaven and hell are true but it is oversimplified. There are numerous planes. After a person dies the soul goes to the plane depending on the person's karma (deeds) and the level of spiritual development. That there are different planes and not just two spirit worlds (heaven and hell) is an opinion which nearly all mediums and psychics unanimously agree upon.

Each plane is meant for a particular type of spiritual evolvement. It is also mentioned by psychics that each plane has various stages within, all earmarking different levels of spiritual evolvement. Thus, on the fourth plane there could be 11 stages. For a soul to move from the fourth plane to the fifth, it will have to first finish all the 11 stages within the fourth plane. After death, an average person who is neither very corrupt nor spiritually advanced moves to the middle plane, the fourth plane on most counts. This depends on numerous facts related to his just concluded life on the physical plane as well as deeds accumulated from other lives. So everything is taken into account: this life, deeds and misdeeds of the just concluded life as well as deeds and misdeeds of the innumerable past lives lived by the particular soul. Most importantly, once the soul takes birth as a human being it does not take rebirth in the animal kingdom. It has to work on its karma being born as a human being. Reincarnation is not restricted to just Hindu philosophy. Most mediums and psychics of different faiths agree on the concept of reincarnation. They are in unison with the fact that we take birth innumerable times due to excessive baggage of deeds; karma.

Swami Sri Sri Yuketswar Giri demarcated the stages, as astral and causal worlds. He divulged that there are numerous worlds, with *Hiranyaloka* (the name might differ due to language), being the ultimate stage in the astral world, after which the soul sheds its astral body and is only cloaked with its causal one. The soul enters the last stage where the idea, the thought reigns. After the causal world, the soul merges with God and becomes God incarnate.

A number of mediums and psychics divide the spirit world into seven stages. The phrase *I felt as though I was in the seventh heaven* seems to sum up the sentiment. After the seventh stage which also has many phases, the soul either moves on to the causal stage or another world. The first stage is dark, cold, dismal, infested with souls who have lived an extremely evil life, filled with harming fellow mankind and other beings and brimming with negative deeds, emotions and with either no redeeming quality or negligible good deeds to account for. These souls live for as long as centuries in such dismal surroundings. What makes it worse is that negative emotions and evil intentions persist in this plane making it a hell. This is hell.

It seems that if the inmates continue harbouring evil and negative thoughts they could be in such a hellhole for eternity. But if a soul repents for its evil life spent on the physical plane, is truly grieved and decides to turn a new leaf, grow spiritually and hope to be forgiven or at least be given a chance to pay for the sins and start afresh, then there is hope. If such a decision is genuine then higher powers and guides take on the responsibility of that particular soul's progress. Yes, one has to pay for one's misdeeds. What is sown must be reaped. You cannot sow weeds and expect to harvest roses. This seems to be the prime law of God; of nature; of His world...all worlds; physical, astral and causal. The soul has to settle accounts but a spirit that wants to be reformed is helped. That itself makes a big difference.

Another point of interest is that progress in the spiritual world is extremely slow and most psychics confirm this aspect in their writings. (A mystery is solved! Government officials, law enforcing authorities, bureaucratic staff, especially in our country obviously still think they are in the spirit world!) As the progress in the spirit world is very slow, where eons can go by before the spirit moves to a higher plane, the soul may wish to return to earth to work out its karma thus moving to higher levels in one birth span on earth. Thus, many souls return to earth to speed up their spiritual progress. But speed has its drawbacks. The soul may return to earth to work on its karma, do noble deeds, accumulate good points, nullify as much as possible its past bad deeds and reach higher levels of consciousness once back in the spirit form. But the catch is that once the soul takes birth, it has no recollection of its noble intentions! Earth has temptations lurking in every corner and opportunities to succumb exist perpetually and man, possessed with a free will and infinite emotions, is constantly at risk of slipping up and sliding ever so low!

The possibility of the soul succumbing to temptations or becoming infested with negative emotions is extremely high. Thus, instead of progressing spiritually, the soul moves further down the spiritual ladder. After death the spirit may realise that its objective to hasten its spiritual journey has backfired. The risk exists and the choice lies between speed and security. (It is somewhat like choosing between making an investment in a bank and buying shares in the stock market. In the former, money invested grows slower than the spirit's growth above. While in the stock market your capital either shoots through the roof or you find yourself signing the bankruptcy form.) That is why many souls prefer to slowly but surely move forward.

Often a soul, to move forward in the spirit world, may decide to work out its karma in one lifetime. It may purposely decide to suffer horrendously in order to wipe clean its karmic slate. It could purposely bring suffering on itself, in the form of either a handicap or an emotional catastrophe. Thus the misconception that a handicap is the sign of sins done in the past lives should be removed. We all are sinners. We all have our bags of karma. Those with handicaps may have purposely chosen such a life to evolve faster and move higher up the spiritual ladder. Only a highly evolved or repentant person will take on such suffering. Only because the soul wants to move faster up the spiritual ladder is such a life on earth chosen. In fact, such souls are even more evolved. The handicap is their choice. No one has forced it upon them. They just want to move faster up the spiritual ladder. Thus, either you have the slow and steady attitude or you come down on earth and throw the dice or take on an extremely heavy cross. The choice is yours.

But is all reincarnation optional? Does the choice ever go out of the soul's hand? What if the soul has no intention of advancing and no intention of returning to the physical plane? What if the soul is enthralled by the plane it finds itself in and is having a ball? It seems that if the blighter is soaking up heavenly delights, least interested in spiritual advancement, then the cool one has no option. The soul then reincarnates. But if the soul is on a very high plane, say sixth or seventh plane where it has got over most of its desires for material pleasures, then reincarnation may be optional.

Back to the spirit world and its stages; after death the soul moves through a metaphysical tunnel and halts at its stage or plane. Here it is met by family and friends passed over earlier. The family and friends may not belong to that same plane. They may belong to a higher plane and may have come to meet their dear ones. The rule of travel being, higher and more advanced souls can travel to lower planes.

We come back to the importance of prayers. Prayers are felt by the soul and prayers help them to progress. Prayers even help the souls to think rationally and wisely. Prayers can also help to give strength, wisdom and a clear perspective to the departed. I say it due to a paranormal experience I have had with a friend.

My wife's friend had committed suicide. I had hardly ever spoken to her but nonetheless we had met often, years before she took her life. Six months after she committed suicide and I had already begun to attend séances, Sai Baba of Shirdi, my presiding guardian angel, informed me the following through automatic writing:

"This friend of yours is going through a very bad time. You had prayed for her soul's peace and spiritual progress but she is listening to no one. She is worried about her child and is repentant of her act, but she is not willing to take my help. Pray for her. Ask God to let her realise that she has passed over. Ask God to let her see reason so that I can help her. Pray for her the Ardibehesht Nirang, every Friday and offer 'sukhard' (sandal wood) in the fire temple. Pray anywhere if you want and any day. Just pray."

I opened the Avesta and the Ardibehesht Nirang sprang before my eyes; a very short prayer. Fortunately I knew it by heart. So I began to pray for this girl, this young mother, who had taken her life so brutally that we, distant friends, still had not been able to come to terms with it. I shudder to think of her family. I prayed whenever I remembered but made it a point to pray every Friday for sure.

A few months later, Sai Baba once again communicated.

"She (Sai Baba wrote her name) is doing well. She is progressing. Thank you for praying for her. Keep up the prayers; they will help her a lot."

I felt nice and warm. That with such a small prayer somebody seemed to be progressing in the spiritual world made me really feel absolutely delighted. Then I read a number of books where it is time and again emphasised that prayers make a major difference for the departed soul. It does not matter in which language you pray. It is important that you beseech God to have mercy on the soul, not let it be earthbound, help the soul to progress and move towards God the merciful. Ask the good Lord to forgive, to love, to guide, to guard and to lead your near and dear departed ones. Ask God to help your loved one to progress spiritually. If the person believed in a particular Prophet or Master, ask God to let that Prophet guide your loved one. Trust me and believe in the numerous confirmations from contacted spirits, prayers help immensely.

So friend, I really advise all to Pray. It really works wonders, not only for those in the spirit world but also for the one saying the prayer.

How far are we dependent on destiny and how much is in the hands of each individual? If everything is predestined then that would mean even our evil actions, intentions, words and designs have been ordained to take place. It applies the same way to righteousness and all that which is Godliness. Is man noble, righteous, kind and charitable because it is destined that he shall be so? Or is it because the man wants to be noble, righteous, kind and charitable as it is the right thing to do and thus shuns everything associated with evil? There are some people who are born with noble intentions. They cannot help doing good, being kind, charitable and righteous. They are genetically cast in such a mould. While there are some who cannot help giving Lucifer a run for the throne, there are many others who have both black and white shades but still through tremendous willpower, walk the straight and Godly path because they sincerely feel that it is best for their souls.

The question is, how important a role does destiny play in our lives, be it good or bad? If all is destined then the man is not really going out of his way to be righteous. He is made to be righteous. Is it possible that if a man is evil may be he is made to be evil? The troubling question is whether Mr. A is selfless, righteous and a pious egg because he cannot help it. He was born selfless, the poor sod and the world's gleefully taking him for one leisurely ride; and Mr. B? He is brimming with evil intent, wants to become a politician and does not mind walking over people and corpses to realise his dream. Is Mr. B destined to give Lucifer sleepless nights or is Mr. B evil because he is weak-willed and lusty for power and money? He is aware that all the lusting for material stuff and power is getting his karmic card a ridiculous score but he cares a damn. He wants to party hard and rough. These are two men. Both contrast by nature. One is treated like a saint and the other like the devil. Are they good and bad because it has been destined so or do they have their priorities in reverse order? All said and done, even priorities differ from people to people. Priorities maketh the man. If the priorities are right your nature and conduct will be right and vice-versa. Is the selection of priorities destined or is it in an individual's hand? I mean, why some men give money priority and some God? Are they made differently or is one an ass and the other wise? Where does destiny stop and individual free will begin is the question? You may say that if one is strong-willed one can achieve the impossible. But even the urge to be strong-willed comes from some inherent vault in one's soul. Some are so strong-willed that if they decide to move a mountain, they will not only shift the mountain but even move a few adjacent peaks just to get their point across. While some others are like this author, so laid-back that even the thought of moving oneself is painful.

With each consequent birth, individual souls shall carry their karma to their next birth: Craft and aptitude, emotions, inclinations, prejudices, likes and dislikes, strengths and weaknesses and inclinations either towards God or towards gold. Thus, destiny in the end too is self-made. Only thing is we are not aware of our past actions and our present karmic intentions. Each time we arrive here it is to better our karmic lot. Most often we take a further plunge down south and go up with a heavier baggage. Once on earth we forget our intention of trying to erase our negative karma and often land doing exactly what one should not be doing. More often than not, we arrive on the physical plane to hasten our spiritual progress. We have decided that it is a must to return to the physical plane in order to move faster in the spirit world, build positive karma and gain a higher place on the spiritual ladder. I repeat, most psychics have insisted that this is one of the sole reasons why we return. But the physical plane is spilling over with temptations of the body and mind. It is also infested with people who should have been safely locked away in a spaceship, with the gas tank half filled and sent rollicking into orbit. A lot of temptation, negativity and hurt come one's way. A lot of misfortune too comes our way making us bitter and negative. What we seem to have forgotten is that these misfortunes have been designed by the person facing them. Only problem is that he or she has forgotten all about karma and erasing of one's negative deeds by undergoing the same suffering we had caused some poor oaf in past lives. The problem is that when we are in the spirit world, we seem to be really in another state of mind, which differs drastically from the one we are in when on earth. So during trouble one looks up to God and curses that He is the cause of all our troubles when in reality poor God has left the entire deal in our own hands. Not only have we designed our lives on earth or the physical plane but also it is we ourselves who have put misfortune in the way so that we can pay off our dues and progress up the spiritual ladder. Only we have forgotten our past actions. So we get further involved in material mire and instead of achieving our objective of a speedy spiritual raise, the plan backfires and the merry-go-round continues. Pain and sorrow mount; frustrations and dejection come one's way; gains and setbacks are all dependent on us and occur due to our past actions and our choice of the necessary steps to rectify them. Nature is just trying its level best to keep the record straight, the slate clean and the accounts to match and be accounted.

Prayers can help the individual to carry his or her cross. Prayers make certain that the cross at least does not get heavier and with time and perseverance the weight gets bearable and eventually the cross no longer exists. Prayers infuse each one of us with positive vibrations and with positive energy; energy that makes every cell thrive; the heart throb and the soul immortal. If one wants help to ease the karmic burden, prayers said with a true heart and mind, with devotion and with selflessness, ensure that help certainly arrives. He has created us. Just like a mother who justifiably gets disappointed but never ever ceases to love, so is Good Old Dad, above.

With prayers our outlook to life improves; outlook towards one's problems changes. We become more positive, calm, steady and level-headed. Faith gets stronger and thoughts more positive. If the person realises that difficulties, hardships, pain, sorrow and agony are necessary for karmic dues to be paid and the slate to get less murky; if he or she accepts the fact and responsibility for such discomfort, the attitude towards facing such calamity changes. Peaceful acceptance enters and frustration, anger and negativity flee. This itself is one of the greatest gifts God can give any of us. I shall be the first to agree that realisation and acceptance of karmic dues is no easy task. When some discomfort enters my life I look up and virtually stop myself from swearing. It is ignorance as well as high-handedness. Often we have the attitude of: "Hey I pray, I am decently righteous, I do not hurt anybody and I have faith in God, then why is misfortune hounding me?" The fact is that we are doing nobody a favour by praying or living a life of a sage. We are doing ourselves; only ourselves a favour. We have forgotten what had transpired in earlier lives. Dues have to be accounted for and what transpires in this life will help us sometime later on, when we throw in the towel and stand twiddling our astral or causal toes in the spirit plane.

I assume that in all natural circumstances you cannot alter what is destined. What prayers can do, I believe, is cushion the impact, give you strength to accept the misfortune and infuse you with optimism, hope and faith that all takes place for the best. That He above, has the reins of your life, firmly in His hands, thus there is nothing to worry about.

I do believe that if one spends more time in meditation and fervent prayers maybe, one can slowly absolve oneself of negative karma. Many yogis believe that through meditation on God, even destiny can be prevented from lashing out to settle accounts. Of course, meditation should be done regularly, effectively and sincerely and for long periods. The same goes for prayers. When you move towards Him, karma gets dispelled. The more you move towards the sun, darkness flees. He is the most luminous sun of all. Brighter than a thousand suns put together. Having a Perfect Master or a Sad-Guru can lighten the baggage of karma. The Master takes on the karma of his faithful and eases his devotees' karmic baggage.

That is why from time immemorial, prayers have been given so much importance by Saints and Sages. When you pray, you infuse your body, mind and soul with God. When you pray, you invoke the very spirit world to make a path for you to reach Him. You dispel negative vibrations and invoke positive ones instead. I know I am repeating the importance of prayers a number of times but its importance can never be overemphasised. It is extremely important. For all, in whichever world one resides, even Vira feels the same.

"Meet Frenny, she will cite you an example of how prayers and Sad-Gurus can make a world of a difference." Vira informed. "Every meeting, Meher Baba and Guru Nanak have repeated the immense power of prayer. When you pray, your communication line with God is switched on. He is listening at the other end. He even speaks to us. But our minds our so clogged with our own problems that we do not hear him. We leave no space for Him to write the message. But if you really listen with devotion, you shall hear Him. He will get His message across and save you from the impending problem."

So all I can say is that if you really want to do yourself a favour, pray. Shut your eyes and communicate with God. Pray for yourself, your family and friends and for those near and dear ones who have left for the spirit world. Ask God to keep you and the clan – on earth and in the spirit world – safe in His arms and protected. Believe me you will be doing a great favour to yourself and your family.

Frenny returned my call and inquired if I wanted a book on Angels. Sure, I said, I would love to read about the most talked about phenomenon in Heaven, angels. I am convinced that angels do exist. But I was far more convinced that children are no angels; even by a long shot at benevolence. This adverse anti-child reaction may have been due to the fact that my son was trying his damn all best to kick his shoe through my shin, through my calf and then kick the ball, which lay behind my leg. Also my daughter was somersaulting from the bed pillar and landing with a loud thud, which must have resulted in my lower-floor neighbours (Good people for certain) to have forsaken the idea of sleep, as all this sombre activity was being conducted at 11.30 at night.

Somehow I managed to conclude the conversation, assuring Frenny that I did not live in a zoo. Then I breathed in deep, put the phone back on the cradle and with a loud yell boxed my son on his ears. At least that is what I thought I wanted to do. My son saw the blow, ducked, boxed me on the family jewels and ran to his sister for safety. I groaned and fell on the floor moaning for dear life. Both my children found the sight of their father moaning on the floor with his feet curled up, extremely hilarious. My children have a wild sense of imagination and assumed I was on the floor entertaining them. So they laughed till tears rushed down their puffy cheeks. If heaven is full of kids then God can keep His heaven. I want no part of it.

The next day was a Sunday and I prepared to leave for Frenny's house in the afternoon.

"Dhatum-dhitum sessions?"

"Ha-ha! "

"Daddy, where you going?" My daughter's attempts at English.

"Dad's going to communicate with ghosts." The wife's attempt at humour.

"Daddy, I want three-three ghosts hun." My son's attempt at mathematics. They began to howl with laughter. Lord, talk about a supportive family!

I rang the door bell and instead of Frenny, another elderly lady opened the door. We introduced ourselves and I approached Frenny who sat on her usual chair with pillows at the back for support.

"As I can no longer read, friends drop by and oblige by reading to me." She handed me the book on Angels.

"I have read the book many years earlier. It is fascinating. My God, how I used to read at a stretch earlier. Hours would pass and I would not get up and put the book down. I must have read virtually all the then available books on spiritualism and the occult...."

"Frenny, have you told him of your experience with Kamu Baba?"

"Ah Kamu Baba!" Frenny's face lit up and even her eyes sparkled. "He was some master. Have you gone to His dargah?"

"No"

"Arrey Ruzbeh you must go. It has such powerful vibrations that if you are a little interested and have the faith in Him, you cannot miss feeling the warmth and pull of His vibrations. I used to go so often when I could see." She sighed. "You know ehn, I went to His dargah the last time? I heard a voice within me saying, 'Kneel down or sit down for a while.' Now kneeling or sitting down on the ground for me is out of question. It is impossible for me to stand up again on my own and anyway my legs cannot take my body weight and my back cannot stand such strain. I tried to avoid the voice but it was persistent. So I sat down with great difficulty. Then the tears began. Like a river they flowed out of my eyes and down my cheeks, wetting the blouse. I cried like I have never done before. I myself could not understand as to why I was crying but tears kept flowing down like a river. Ah, Kamu Baba is some Master."

According to Frenny, Kamu Baba was the disciple of Sad-Guru Sai Baba of Shirdi (my Guru as well). When Kamu Baba was young, He used to live with Sai Baba. Kamu Baba then settled down in Bombay; Goregaon to be precise. He lived all His life in Goregaon. When not praying or being with His disciples, HE would spend His time in His garden.

"I was introduced to Him in the year 1947-48 when I was a very young woman. I did not believe in Babas and only had faith in my religion. But I went to see Him just out of curiosity for I had never visited a Baba. But the moment He saw me He inquired as to why I was not wearing a sudra and kusti? He also revealed a number of matters that were very private and only known to my family. I was shocked at how this stranger had known that I was not wearing the sudra and kusti, as well as about intimate family details. From then onwards I became an ardent follower of Kamu Baba and began to frequent Him for blessings very regularly. He used to always call me Muii (a playful way of calling a woman who you know well and like).

"In the year 1969, May 15 or May 16, my husband was admitted into the ICU of a hospital due to cerebral haemorrhage. In 1969, science was not as advanced as it is now, so in those days this meant certain death. I was not in Bombay but in Ahmedabad when my husband was in the ICU. I could not stay by his bedside as he was in the ICU. I rushed to Kamu Baba's residence. Those days there were few people around and we could meet Him without a problem. He blessed me and said, 'Muii, why have you come so late?' Then He inquired as to my husband's age. I told Him (he was 57 years old). Kamu Baba did not say anything for a while. Then he sighed and told me that He could not do anything for my husband as his time to leave the physical plane had arrived. I just caught His feet and began to weep and begged Him to help my husband live. I had a small daughter, I was all alone, I was still young and I could not live without my husband's love and support. He kept saying that there was no way He could make my husband live but I was adamant. I threatened that I would not leave till He had given me His assurance.

"After a lot of persuasion, He sighed and asked me to wait. Then He went into the prayer room and after a short while returned. He told me that though my husband's time had arrived but maybe there was a small chance to prolong his stay. He then told me that the next '18 days are very critical for your husband. But he should be alive to see the dawn of the 11th morning. Once he survives the 10th day, Muii your husband will live.' Then He told me that I should pray:

*'Jal tu, jalal tu, sahebey kamal tu,
mushkil khusha tu, aai bala tal tu'.*"

"He said that I should go on saying this short prayer but on the 10th day the moment I feel his health deteriorating I should sit by his side and continuously say this prayer. Not once should I even get up. Then Baba told me to immediately get a 18 by 18 piece of white cloth, put one fist of grain into it and a small coin, then to put the cloth under my husband's pillow and in the morning give the cloth to the first servant who entered the room."

"You can imagine the difficulty in getting an 18 by 18 piece of white cloth at 11 O'clock at night. But somehow we managed to find a tailor's shop open. The tailor believed in my urgency and obliged. In the morning we gave the cloth with grain and coin to the first servant who came into the room. My husband began to recover. In fact even the doctors were surprised at my husband's recovery. The 10th day arrived. Ironically, all morning he was much better than ever before. I heaved a sigh of relief but at the back of my mind I remembered Kamu Baba's words that the 10th day would be the most critical. It would decide whether I was going to become a widow and my child fatherless. Exactly at two in the afternoon my husband's health deteriorated. One moment he was fine and the next moment he was gasping for breath and fighting for life. He was sinking. I sat by his bed and began to say the prayer my Kamu Baba had given to me. All through the day and all through the night I sat by the side of my husband and prayed. Not once did I get up. Not once. The doctors gave up hope. They were certain that he would no longer survive. But I kept my faith in Kamu Baba and prayed. Exactly at dawn, slowly my husband's condition began to improve. By the afternoon of the 11th day he was much better. Those doctors who were certain of my husband not seeing the morning were shocked to find him alive when they returned to work. One of the top surgeons admitted that my husband was not saved either by doctors or by science. He agreed that God and my Kamu Baba were responsible for my husband's life. My husband lived for nine more years. He expired in 1978 while it was in 1969 that he had nearly died." Frenny sighed and looked beyond me at the past gone by: "I had two miscarriages. I told my plight to Baba, He blessed me and in a short while I got pregnant and the delivery went safely."

"Who was Kamu Baba?"

"Kamu Baba was the disciple of Sai Baba of Shirdi. Sai Baba is your Guardian Angel, isn't it so?"

"Yes." I humbly acknowledged. "Why don't you call Kamu Baba during the séance?"

"He has come a few times but unfortunately the mediums are keener to communicate only with their Guides so they do not encourage Kamu Baba. In 1990, I had nearly become blind. Virtually there was darkness. The light was slowly extinguishing. In fact, I had reached a stage of near blindness. I could see nothing though there was very little light left. On Saturdays we go to 'G' School for the séance. Those days our Phiroze Kapadia used to conduct the sessions. Oh how I wish you had met Phiroze when he was well. He was the best medium ever. I have met many but none compared to Phiroze. The lectures he used to give while in a trance were gems of wisdom. Now Tara holds the classes. So in 1990, I was in the séance when Kamu Baba's spirit entered one of the mediums. Usually when a medium goes into a trance, he or she walks around, stops near the person for whom the message is and delivers it. So the medium in a trance with Kamu Baba's spirit walked around and halted in front of me. 'Kem Muii, how fat you have become.' Hearing the word Muii after so many years I got tears in my eyes. I said: 'what to do Kamu Baba, I have become blind so I cannot go out. All day I am at home. I am confined to the house with nothing to do.' Kamu Baba chuckled through the medium and said: 'So you wake up in the middle of the night and eat biscuits.' You can imagine how shocked I was. How did Kamu Baba know such details? I felt so nice and comforted that He still kept a watch over me. Then Kamu Baba through the medium began to heal my failing eyes. Through the medium HE began to massage the area around my eyes. Fingers gently massaged the skin next to my eyes. Slowly I could make out that the darkness was decreasing. I could see light more clearly and through certain angles I could see hazy outlines of people around me. But unfortunately the mediums wanted to speak to their respective Guides. Unfortunately for me, it was the first and last time Kamu Baba came to the Saturday session. In just one sitting my eyesight became so much better. I am certain with just another one or two sittings Kamu Baba would have cured me of my blindness."

This explained why Frenny often tilted her head up and looked sideways. The healing done by Kamu Baba enabled Frenny from virtually blind to see more of light and even shadows, amazing!

"From complete blindness now I can see shadowy outlines. I can know if the light is on. If I had seen you before I had lost my sight, then meeting you again, through part memory, part shadowy sight, I would have made out your appearance. You my son are a shadow. But if you get up or move about I can follow you up to a distance."

"But why didn't you insist on allowing Kamu Baba to heal you and communicate with you?"

"See, mediums are interested in their Guides, those whom they know intimately. In fact, when once Kamu Baba had come on Vira's board, He had told me that He did not come for the Saturday sessions, as no one wanted Him; He wanted to communicate but could not without some medium wanting Him to come through. In the entire group I am the only one who knows Kamu Baba."

Later on when I spoke to Vira she also mentioned her sole visit to Kamu Baba.

"I met Him only once. I went to meet Him and He said that he knew my father very well. I was surprised as I had not mentioned about my father and no one knew me in His group. But such souls know everything beforehand. Then Kamu Baba told me that I would lose the court case. I should not pursue it. I would incur a very bad financial loss if I would continue with the case. I was very impressed, as I had not spoken a word about the case to anyone. He just knew beforehand why we had gone to meet Him. But I still went ahead with the case. As He had predicted, I really lost the court case and went into a big financial loss. As I had not listened to Him I felt very odd to meet Him again. That was the first and last time I met Kamu Baba."

I inquired with Frenny how Kamu Baba expired. For some reason, I felt very close to this humble but great Master. For some reason He had touched a chord within me. Also that He was Sai Baba's devotee and disciple made the bonding more intense.

"What happens with these great souls is that They take upon Themselves the suffering of Their followers. They take upon themselves the karma of Their devotees. Baba's health began to deteriorate as He took more and more on Himself. They not only heal others but actually take on their sufferings upon Themselves. The strain of bearing the karma of devotees becomes too much and that is why in the end They leave the physical plane and continue to take upon Themselves the karma of devotees but in the spirit form.

"I can walk about now because my Guide is Swami Narayan who though still in the flesh heals me through the spirit. Earlier, I used to be awakened every day at four in the morning with a warm feeling starting from my feet and permeating through my body. I was being healed. But then like a fool I began to tell everyone and so the healing stopped. But even now I go to the Saturday session where I am given healing. Without these healing sessions I would be bedridden. Even the doctors wonder how I walk about and am not on bed permanently. They will not understand that I have a very powerful doctor working on me, my Swami Narayan. My daughter was diagnosed to be suffering from leukaemia...blood cancer. My Swami Narayan, through my niece, who is a devoted follower of Him, gave my daughter something to eat. The next morning while passing her motions, a huge, fat wart, red with blood came out with her stool. After that she became all right. The doctors were shocked when they saw her new blood report. There was not a trace of leukaemia. My Swami Narayan saved my daughter.

"My entire life I have gone through a lot of suffering but have been blessed with God and miracles. Before I forget, you must meet Zarina and hear her story. Her case is virtually a miracle. She is living because Sai Baba, your Guardian Angel has been healing her. That she is living today is a miracle."

I finished the mint tea and left for home, a humbled man. There is so much more to life yet we throw it away lusting for things that really do not matter. All through our lives we run after moronic pursuits when heaven waits for us to look beyond the false glitter of gold at the real glow of God. There is so much of substance to really run after but we squander our lives chasing mirages and shadows when God and His Angels stand by, wondering and mourning at our foolishness.

I reached home expecting the kids to be sleeping. All adults were fast asleep, but the kids were wide-awake. The adults lay flat on their stomachs, defeated.

"They have been spanked, yelled at and apart from flogging, everything was done to them but to no avail…"

"Dhaddy, mummy hitten me on my trhee-trhee putt-putt." Pashaan informed. Putt-putt means buttocks in child lingo.

"Ahhh yes. Curly you come here and you my fat plum pudding, Vahishta sleep with vanquished adults of the house."

We lay down and I wondered if Meher Castillino had a book on the power to heal. I wanted to read more….

"Daddy, I'm hungry…"

"I also wanting to eat….Vahishta don't eat my Perk…" I heard a loud groan from the adults.

In India we know that God-realised souls, seeped into God and nothing else, have cured and healed countless devotees suffering from fatal diseases. In the book Sai Charitra, there are innumerable recorded cases of devotees being cured of fatal illnesses by Sai Baba of Shirdi. Even after Sai Baba shed his physical cloak, He has performed miracles that defy the laws of medicine and science for those devotees who have lived with true faith and devotion and loved and looked up to Sai Nath.

God incarnates like Sai Baba of Shirdi, Meher Baba and Kamu Baba, Guru Nanak, Zarathustra, Jesus Christ and the few and far between God Men and Prophets and Avatars that have blessed the earth with Their presence have not only cured devotees suffering from fatal illnesses but have averted even those ailments that are in one's destiny and have yet to affect the devotee. For such evolved souls who can alter destiny, curing devotees of terminal diseases is but a small feat.

Many who suffer from fatal diseases have been saved by God realised souls, who through spiritual powers could bring about such wonders. But there are certain healers who cure people of fatal diseases but are neither Saints nor have spiritual prowess, but can do so due to God realisation. Most often they are ordinary people, with singularly ordinary lifestyles, which include marriage, who are blessed by Providence with the power to heal people suffering from pain and disease. They are blessed. Maybe their deeds in their past lives had been related to such a gift thus resulting in an outburst of what seems a miraculous ability to heal in this life.

Ruth Montgomery's book, *The Greatest Healer Of Our Time*

is of great importance for a number of reasons. The healer who is identified as Mr. Philip A had no education either as a doctor or as a healer. Since childhood he had this miraculous gift of healing ill people. He was born with the gift to heal, handed to him on a platter by benevolent Providence as well as by his own karmic tendencies.

According to Mr. A, the power to heal is simple. It is the Ancient Wisdom of generating human energy to match each person's energy frequency. It sure is simple. When energy is not prevalent or has decreased due to whatever reason, illness arises. The intensity of the illness is in direct proportion to the lack of energy in that afflicted area.

Thus, not only does Mr. A have no medical qualification, he does not beseech God to heal. "He works by recharging and revitalising what he calls the human magnetic field or the master brain, which distributes energy to all parts and functions of the body. Laying his ears to a patient's chest, he occasionally says aloud 'Oh, I've got the signal.' As he listens, the vibrations reveal to him the body tensions and the location of nerve centres which are in spasm. Then by placing his fingers on certain areas, he generates the particular energy which blends with the individual's and the correction is usually affected within a matter of minutes," informs Ruth.

Mr. A follows his inner guidance. He terms the force that generates the guidance as 'The Power of Powers'. The amazing aspect of Mr. A, like George Anderson, the psychic medium, is that he too is not certain how he hears the body tension and how he performs the recovery; often miraculous recoveries. "There is no such thing as a miracle. What seems so, results from the correct application of natural laws. A miracle is simply what one does not yet understand."

Philip A has cured people suffering from cancer, heart ailments, crippling arthritis and other equally life-threatening and painful afflictions. His explanation as to why these problems occur and how he amends them and brings the body back to normal are amazing.

According to Mr. A the life-force (that sustains life and keeps each part of the body in perfect condition) is electrical energy. Our bodies are constructed to conduct and transmit the human energy current. His reply to what is cancer is revealing. "This is what has been explained to me over the air since my earliest memory. When the tissue doesn't receive the necessary life energy, then a weaker section of the tissue begins to deteriorate; shutting itself off from energy; the tissue dies and gas forms in the cells, causing bloating and expansion. Because of a low energy level, the live cells don't have the resistance to slough off the dead ones, so the dead cells destroy the live ones. It's something like one bad apple in a barrel gradually causing all the others to rot. When this condition exists, any shock or insult to the body further weakening it, will intensify and speed up the deterioration process. When the energy is brought up to capacity to strengthen the live cells so that they are able to fight the dead cells, the dead cells will slough off, unless the malignancy is in the final stages. The dead cells ordinarily have a tendency to disintegrate, sometimes sloughing off like strings."

All ailments, according to this powerful healer, are caused because the magnetic field does not pull enough energy from the air breathed into the lungs to supply to the different parts of the body. If a section does not get the required energy, problems occur. The less the energy received, the graver the health problem.

"A stroke too has its origins in the magnetic field. It can be avoided by previously releasing the spasm that has built up in the magnetic field, through feeding human energy currents to the proper one."

"Arthritis is caused due to failure in energy distribution. Energy is distributed to each organ of the body and calcium is normally circulated throughout our bodies in liquid form. If energy is not distributed properly, the calcium which is in liquid form solidifies in the weakest sections such as joints and at points of sluggish nerves. Nerves in contact with this solidified calcium develop pain and irritation and as the deposits build up, the joints become frozen and immobile. Healing energy is sent to these hardened calcium areas and the deposits begin to soften and crumble and gradually the waste is flushed through the kidneys and bladder. In minutes the pain becomes less and in a few sittings the arthritis is gone."

Two important points raise their silly heads. One is how does Mr. A diagnose an illness without being told of the problem; and second how does he go about functioning as a hyperactive power station?

When asked from where he gets the information and diagnosis, Mr. A informs, "From tuning in on The Ring." According to the healer, a protective ring of energy circles each planet and stores within it all knowledge since time immemorial. Thus, not only does this ring of energy store knowledge but it also protects the planet from colliding and hurtling itself without direction, into the cosmos.

A similar concept is adopted by Zoroastrians all over the world. Zoroastrians wear a thread made out of the fine hair of a white lamb called the *kusti* on a specially designed vest made out of muslin, called the *sudreh*. The *kusti* is a flattened tube of white wool about 1/4 inch in width. It has 72 strands interwoven in it, each strand standing for a chapter in the *Yasna*, the high liturgy of Zoroastrianism. The *kusti* is tied during the recitation of the *Zend Avesta* prayers. Just as each planet has a protective ring of energy around it, every religion treats each individual as a universe by himself and each Zoroastrian ties the *kusti* around the waist as a protective ring for his or her universe. Tied while reciting the prayers devotionally, the vibrations create a protective ring around the person: An invisible ring similar to the invisible ring that is around each planet in the cosmos. I find it amazing that this tradition has been in use before the advent of Zarathustra, who Himself blessed the earth with His presence more than 1500 years before Christ.

Ruth Montgomery's book, *The Greatest Healer Of Our Time*, makes fascinating reading. Not once did I doubt the power of Mr. A. He is certainly a man gifted by God and one so blessed can truly perform miracles. No two ways about it. Below is an extract from the same book:

> "For as long as I (Mr. A) remember, I was receiving a continual flow of information coming over the air from The Universal Ring of Wisdom, explaining the Ancient Wisdom of life, and I was receiving instructions pertaining to the generation of human energy. Receiving this information was always as constant and natural to me as breathing but it was puzzlement to my family...."

> "The theory of energy as the life-force and body activity is as old as the ages," he continues, "and there are many well-versed in the Ancient Wisdom to whom most of this is known. This world we live in is composed of gases and energy. All substances – plant, animal and human life – result from the unlimited combination of energy frequencies acting on these gases. Every plant, animal and human has its own individual energy frequency to establish and maintain life, growth and development. At birth, the first breath of life is our direct supply, our lifeline with the Universal Power....Life itself! At any time this energy flow is cut off from the magnetic field, the energy which originally sets the field becomes a part of the Power it came from. So long as this energy is established and flows through without obstruction, we are in tune with the Universal supply of energy."

Mr. A says that in the lower abdomen is the master brain, an intricate system forming the magnetic field, *"The grouping together of the main trunk nerves with its branches and relay systems extending throughout the entire body."* Normally, he explains, the magnetic field gives the lungs the strength to pull in all the energies. But the field in turn draws its personal energy frequency from the lungs to itself, for distribution throughout the body. He says that some of the symptoms of insufficient energy distribution are shortness of breath, nervousness, confusion, restlessness, irritability, bloating, pain and a feeling of heaviness. Their intensity depends on the degree of depletion of the magnetic field, which is caused by fear, anger, hatred, shock or improper or deficient nerve fuelling.

> "A child is born with a strong or a weak nervous system," he says, "which is determined at conception and is the result of his parent's energies. If the mother and father are of mated frequencies and are well and strong at the time the child is conceived, that child ordinarily has an easy birth and a strong, healthy nervous system. If the child is the result of mismatched energy currents and the future parents are nervous, discontented, or unhealthy, the baby usually has a weak nervous system – the delivery too may be difficult. Because of this, he is the victim of low energy and nerve depletion for most of his life. But even when a child inherits a weak magnetic field, that tension can be released shortly after birth by someone with the properly blended energy who is able to convey this energy to the infant's magnetic field so that the infant is freed from bondage and is open to the universe and is thereby able to draw his normal capacity of energy from the atmosphere."

Mr. A insists that too much exposure to the sun can be

dangerous. Apart from skin cancer and depletion (caused due to sunbathing) the sun saps energy from the body. "The sun pulls water out of lakes and streams, what do you think it does to your body? If clothed, a person exposed to it receives energy. Otherwise it causes dehydration and depletion of energy in people exposed to its rays."

Mr. A emphasises that all thoughts, inventions and knowledge, are *"taken off the Ring."* The only problem is our ability to tune in. We should not be surprised that when tuned in, vibrations in the air can bring forward pictures that converse and make private communication between two individuals possible, even if they be separated by oceans. Our forefathers had never dreamt and would have denounced the possibility of two people communicating with each other from two different ends of the earth or watching events unfold that are taking place at the same time thousands of miles away in a country whose name you can barely pronounce.

Television, telephone, cell phone, the net and man strolling on the moon, reaching it through a flying machine that weighs the Lord alone knows how many tons is now not given a second thought. Electrical devices that aid communication and are a medium to entertain us function through the same principle through which Mr. A picks up his information. If you and I can communicate through the cell phone that has no wires attached, thousands of miles away from each other, why can't people receive messages from an invisible ring that surrounds our planet?

Inventions in electronics and science were not thought possible centuries ago but are now taken for granted and a world without the telephone and television seems not only impractical but even impossible. Knowledge is present in The Ring, but our minds are not tuned in. Though we have the ability to communicate unaided, our skill has diminished owing to dormancy of our spiritual prowess through the innumerable lives we have lived.

The knowledge is and the Ring moves about oblivious to its invisibility, but mankind due to a shift in priorities no longer can tune into the vault of knowledge. There are individuals, however, who with interest only in God may still have the facility to tune into such matters. In India, through meditation in Vedic times, man could achieve the impossible as the power of the mind then was intact. Mahabharata and the Ramayana are filled with stories of miracles. Astral projection, gravity being shamelessly ignored, thought projection, communication with Gods and Goddesses, healing through touch and walking on water, all this, to many people are just myths.

They are not. God Incarnates, with yogic powers can defy gross physical laws for they belong to a realm beyond the physical world. In *The Autobiography Of A Yogi*, by Sri Paramhansa Yogananda, there are innumerable examples of how through yoga, what seem to be miracles are simple feats performed by yogis, without batting an eyelid.

The Bible describes more than a hundred psychic phenomena. All ancient books mention conversation with God, Angels and Spirits. In Holy Books, miracles are not exceptions but the order of the day. In those days people lived for a long, long time. Why? Because they knew the Ancient Wisdom, lived a wise, sensible and a God-fearing life and avoided reading health magazines. Nothing is impossible. The fact is what seems impossible now was possible then and what seemed impossible then is mundane stuff now.

One of the least familiar methods of communicating with the spirit world as well as confirming the fact that there are other dimensions existing parallel to ours is through the humble tape recorder. When I divulged to my family the fact that we could communicate with spirits through the tape recorder, they gave up on the dim hope of my behaving normal and attributed my utterings to a temporary loss of reason.

"This is no temporary loss of reason. He has gone insane. I think the fact that nobody wants an editor seems to have snapped all coordination between body and brain…"

"What brain? The chap has been walking about, a menace to family and friends without even pretending he has a brain, otherwise would he dare say things like contacting spirits through a tape recorder?"

If family and friends are karmic gear, carried about with oneself for the rest of eternity, boy am I in trouble? Their support and constant encouragement has been so short in supply – and when supplied I wished they had refrained from it – that I am sincerely going to address the matter to the Lord above, the moment I have dropped this battered body.

Anyway, the fact is that spirit communication is possible even through the means of electronic devices. Vira has since long been telling me that both Meher Baba as well as Guru Nanak insist that sometime soon communication shall be coming through the telephone and other electronic devices as well. "As time draws nearer when most of mankind will be destroyed, the spirit world will try its best to make man change his ways."

The most fascinating point regarding communicating with spirits through the electronic media is that there are no set rules. Some researchers have succeeded in establishing contact with spirits through extremely sophisticated equipment in sound-proof recording studios. But then there are some who have used a normal but effective audio system to achieve similar success. The most important need for establishing contact with spirits through such a medium is that there should be silence when the recording is being done. Silence, a decent set of audio equipment and the desire to establish contact are the only components required for such a mode of spirit communication. So once the equipment is set up and the room ensured of silence, the person desirous of establishing contact should first beseech the spirit he or she wants to establish contact with. If one is desirous of just establishing contact with any spirit then an open invitation to spirits to use the recorder to voice their thoughts should be made. "I would like to communicate with evolved, God-loving spirits. Please speak to me through this recorder." Something like this should be said and then the recorder switched on for 10 to 15 minutes. After the lapse of such time, switch off the tape, rewind it and then play it and listen, preferably through ear phones. Try to hear the recorded cassette for a few times. Often on first hearing one may not discern anything but who knows one may be lucky on the third hearing? When you are absolutely sure that the tape is blank, repeat the exercise. You never know when contact may be made. If I were you, I would light a diva, burn incense sticks, pray to God and then commence trying to contact spirits. I am certain you are interested in contacting noble spirits.

This got me interested and after a lot of effort I got my hands on a wonderful book written by Harold Sherman, the author of the immensely popular *You Live After Death* with the book in my hand, *The Dead Are Alive*. In it there is an excellent chapter devoted to communicating with the spirit world through the tape. In fact there is even a term to this method "Electronic Voice Phenomena", I quote from the book:

> *"In 1959, Friedrich Jurgenson, of Molubo, Sweden while recording 'bird sounds' in a forest, was astounded when he played back the tape, to find human voices on it, one of which appeared to be his long deceased mother's voice. He heard his own name called and the words, 'Friedrich, you are being watched'. The more he listened, the more he became convinced that these sounds were not radio signals; they were coming through on tape in different languages – Swedish, German or Latvian."*

Jurgenson concluded that these voices had to be emanating from another Dimension. Before making his discovery public, however, he devoted four years to careful and systematic experimentation, during which time he recorded several thousand voices. He encountered interference with what is called 'white sound', through which the voices had to emerge, some exceptionally faint or in whispers and occasionally loud and easy to hear, often establishing their identity as entities who had formerly lived on earth.

Two of the pioneer investigators in the United States were the Lamoreaux brothers, Joseph and Mike, of Washington State. In their experimentation, they also recorded some thousands of voices and received many messages as answers to questions, which they carefully and systematically recorded for future checking and evaluation. When a friend, Jim Remich, was accidentally killed, they were able to contact him after some time, and in one communicative session, they asked him if there were any Rules for Living, like our 'Ten Commandments', where he was.

'Yes, there are,' was Jim's recorded reply. *'If you will*

leave your tape running, I will try to give them to you.'
The Lamoreaux Brothers did as directed and these are
the exact words, which appeared on the tape.
'There are Six rules.
The First Rule is to live as though you are part of everyone.
The Second Rule is to help everyone.
The Third Rule is to not let anyone feel alone.
The Fourth Rule is to love everyone.
The Fifth Rule is to forgive everyone.
The Sixth Rule is to live like you are one with everyone
and everyone is one with God.'

Amazing! I also learnt another important thing about the spirit world, communicating with spirits and the importance of prayers. It seems that a certain gentleman by the name of AJ lost his wife, Wilma Plimpton on December 10, 1974. (December 10 seems to ring a bell. The date seems ominous. What could it be? Ah yes, it's my wedding anniversary!) Anyway, Wilma Plimpton expired and when finally she was able to establish communication with her much grieving husband (though after many months) she revealed that after she passed over she found herself in another hospital. The first thought was that her husband had shifted her to some new clinic but when she saw her parents, at first she assumed she was dreaming. It took some time for her parents to convince her that she was really dead and at the moment in a Rest Home, one of many such homes, which exist around the earth, where most dead folk are kept for some time, the duration depending on the spirit's eagerness to adapt to its new surroundings.

All throughout, Wilma was overwhelmed by the emotional pull of her husband, mourning her death. She responded to his call of grief and found herself in the astral body in their home in Oklahoma and in front of her grieving husband, who sat staring at her photograph. The amazing thing was that though she had no idea then how she managed to reach her husband in the wink of an eye, the fact was that there she was sitting in front of him trying to comfort him and attract his attention towards her which was naturally unsuccessful.

AJ meanwhile was contemplating on ending his life. The death of his wife had robbed the very essence and meaning out of his existence. Then by chance and as fate would have it, he came across Harold Sherman's *You Live After Death*. AJ contacted the author and they met. Harold Sherman then explained to the widower the various ways and means of communicating with the spirit world. As AJ was well versed in electronics and his son was an electronic engineer with NASA, naturally Sherman recommended that AJ experiment with the Electronic Voice Phenomena.

It took AJ three months of exhaustive attempts before he could record a single voice on his tape and then the voices began to flow in. In his own words to Sherman: "But I can't make out who they're," he said. "I've begun to get a lot of them like a crowd at Grand Central Station….every one trying to talk at once….some voices are too faint to understand…others are in whispers…and some are loud enough to hear plainly against the static. I don't know why it took so long before I could get any voices at all but I've sure got them now. No doubt about that!"

What AJ was hearing were the voices of 'earthbound souls'. Earthbound souls are those souls who for various reasons have still not let go the bond with the earth. Very often people refuse to accept the fact that they have left their physical bodies and are no longer part of the physical world but are now new entrants in the spirit world. They refuse to accept that life exists in other dimensions. They obdurately cling to their conviction that they are not dead but still living in their former bodies and what they are observing all around them is nothing but a dream or a nightmare, depending on the stage of spiritual evolution. Thus, the soul remains earthbound. The other reason why a soul remains earthbound is its obsessive attachment to earth and the physical plane. It is so obsessed with material pleasures and desires that it remains close to its source. Many times souls just do not understand what is going on around and are not willing to take help of guides who are sent to help them cross over. They are confused and due to a lack of knowledge about the existence of other dimensions and the spirit world, they spend years wandering about aimlessly. Also excessive grief, anger, lust, hate and revenge make the soul remain earthbound. For some reason, I still have not been able to grasp, it is easier for us in the physical plane to help earthbound souls realise the folly of their behaviour as well as help them cross over. Maybe when a Guide or a Guardian Angel tries to convince the adamant earthbound soul to cross over to the spirit world, the confused soul still assumes that it is just a dream. But when a psychic medium or folk like you and me, (who really wish the earthbound souls to find peace and live in harmony in the land of sunshine and God), pray aloud, speaking clearly to the earthbound souls (who can see and hear us), that they are truly dead and that salvation for them lies in the fact that they take the help of evolved souls to move on, the chances of them heeding advice is great. Evolved souls are present whenever a soul decides to take help. The important point is, the individual spirit should take a firm stand and decide to get its earthbound ass out of the dismal surroundings.

For instance, AJ was beseeched by earthbound souls who "were calling for help…they seemed to be in a confused state… some could not remember their identity…some did not know they had died…some could not tell where they were…they were surrounded by darkness and gloom…they were in a dream or nightmarish state…and they did not know how to get out of it…"

Often the earthbound soul would pretend that it was DJ's

Wilma, just to draw his attention but when quizzed they would admit defeat. At long last the real Wilma did make contact.

I find it strange as well as humble to realise that the human heart has such power that it can change, alter and reform the laws of nature if really, a true-to-GOD desire exists. Also, the fact that spirits yearn to communicate and utilise different means to make their voices get through is fascinating as well as sad.

Often, earthbound souls communicate with mediums in the guise of the soul contacted. You may think you are communicating with your departed near and dear one but in reality it may be some other spirit who may have taken over just in order to communicate with the medium. Thus, it is best that extremely intimate questions are asked which no one but the deceased would be aware of. Also for those who are into spirit communication, it is imperative that you say prayers, light an incense stick or a diva, or sit in front of the Deity whom you worship. Make sure the force of prayers protects you from any deranged spirit trying to take you for a helluva ride. Life can be hell if the right precaution is not taken. I certainly recommend that you try and communicate with only a known spirit and not any spirit lingering about. Do not invite trouble by trying to be a grand host. It can cost you your sanity or even your life. If you are not confident about yourself then sit in a group, chant prayers and before you begin say aloud many times the word Om. This all-powerful word cleanses the environment, paves the path for noble spirits and makes certain that troublesome spirits are kept at bay. Whatever you may do, make sure you have said your prayers buddy.

Earthbound souls exist in every family. Your loved ones could be hovering earthbound for decades in a state of limbo which is in a way, worse than the lowest spiritual plane as the state of limbo can be for all eternity and thus, there is no scope for spiritual evolvement and evolution. The best way one can help family and friends who are earthbound souls (of this life and those from one's past lives) is to pray that the earthbound soul moves on with his or her spiritual journey. Pray to GOD to give these souls peace of mind and wisdom and help them to become aware that they are really in the spirit world and not in a state of dreams. Pray that evolved Guides come and take these earthbound souls to their respective spiritual dimensions from which progress is possible. Pray for all earthbound souls to move towards GOD and light. Even if you can help a few earthbound souls through the power of your prayers, you will have made a real difference not only to their lives but even to yours. There are earthbound souls who cling to their near and dear ones, well aware that they are dead and in the spirit world. These earthbound souls are either so possessive of their family and friends that even death cannot do them apart. Or they want to live their incomplete lives and satiate their incomplete desires through folk on planet earth. This causes immense agony and hardship for the person on earth, who is being clung on to by the earthbound soul.

Astrologers have often been baffled as to why a person seems not to make any worldly progress when the horoscope is so grand that success and wealth are assured. But instead only failure and poverty are habitual confidants. What the astrologers often do not take into account is that many times an earthbound soul is clinging on to his client. That turns the horoscope into a horror-scope. Only prayers in such instances help. So buddy, it's my advice that you spare a thought for the earthbound souls in your daily prayer, not only for their welfare but who knows, maybe even for yours.

Throughout my conversations with both Vira and Frenny, the mention of Zarina Messman's miraculous recovery when all had given her up for dead was repeatedly mentioned. I had met Zarina in the séance sessions also. She certainly did not look the type who had returned from the jaws of death. She looked healthy and strong. I phoned her and she was only too eager to be of any help towards the book. I spoke aloud to the family.

"All of them go out of their way to help me…"

"Naturally"

"What's so natural…"

"They want you out of their lives as early as possible."

The wife and her corny humour. I put on the old jeans, loose shirt and was about to leave when I passed my mother.

"Where are you going?"

"I am going to speak to a fellow group member…"

"You are dressed as though you are going to scare some shopkeeper to pay you protection money. Please, first brush your hair, trim your beard and look civilized."

"Forget it mom, why expect the impossible from your son. Looking civilized is out of his power…yes physical and your so called astral…"

"One of these days I shall for sure die with such humour making the rounds." With my family such as this, who needs publishers and politicians to make life miserable?

I reached Zarina's place and made certain that my hair was not pointing up north. She opened the door and inquired as to whether I had lost my way trying to find the house. By force of habit I was going to reply in the affirmative but checked myself. No, I had not got lost at least this time. Bombay and I never really are at home with each other.

I give below Zarina Messman's story in her own words on how she was cured by her Guardian Angels, Sai Baba and Meher Baba. (Her story was also featured in a popular magazine. Zarina had narrated the story to Meher Castillino, former Miss India, model, fashion critic and an extremely kind-hearted and generous woman without whose support and the books lent by her to the author, it would have been extremely difficult to have written this book.) I reproduce below Zarina's story:

"Religion has always played an important part in my life and as a child I had several spiritual experiences. When I was eight-nine-years-old (though I was not aware of it then) I had these out-of-body experiences when asleep. I would fly over hills, rivers and lakes and then with a thud I would return to my body. After each such experience I used to be terribly frightened. It was natural. I was still a child and I just did not understand what was happening to me. But today my life is led according to the Will of my two spiritual Guides, Sai Baba and Meher Baba, who have given me a new reason to live."

"Since childhood, I have led a difficult life but I had no major health problems; school, a psychology degree and a job in a bank followed. Health-wise minor problems, like cough and colds prompted the removal of my tonsils at the age of 24. But little did I foresee that my health would cause me such torment and pain and finally lead me to a new way of life and thinking."

"In 1984 at the age of 40, I experienced acute gynaecological problems. A sonographic examination revealed fibroids, which were immediately removed. The doctor warned me then that should the fibroids recur I would have to go in for hysterectomy. For three years my health was alright but slowly it began to deteriorate. In 1992 my abdomen, face and hands bloated and the pain was so excruciating that even painkillers did not help. Everything pointed to a hysterectomy. I argued it could be due to menopause and thus held off the operation."

"Finally I decided on the surgery. A month prior to the operation I had very severe cough. My gynaecologist suggested I suppress it with medicine but it did not work. My doctor assured me that all would go well. I was admitted at 8.30 pm the night before the procedure. I had a very hearty meal that night. Before sleeping I was given around six injections to suppress the cough. The following day, i.e., on November 8, 1993 at 9.30 am, I was wheeled into the Operation Theatre."

"After the four-hour surgery, fibroids and a bulky uterus that weighed as much as a two-and-a-half-month child were removed. Recovering from the anaesthesia, I kept murmuring that my throat hurt a lot. My family thought I was delirious since I had been operated on the stomach and there was no connection between the throat and the operation. When the effect of the anaesthesia wore off, I once again complained that my throat hurt badly. My family was baffled since I should have been in reality complaining of a stomach-ache. Nurses gave me water since I had not had anything to drink for 24 hours. The moment I took a sip I felt as though my throat was aflame. The burning sensation, as the drops of water went down my throat was unbearable. The doctor explained that a tube had been inserted in my throat during the operation – thus the soreness. Everything would be fine within a few days he assured me. But I could swallow water with great difficulty, leave aside pills or food. Milk diluted with water was given too but I would vomit it out along with a thick white sticky froth that kept pouring out of my throat and mouth. Eight days later I was discharged from the hospital. The doctor said that I would be fine at home and if I had a problem I should go to an ENT specialist. When I visited one, I could hardly talk to him. The sticky white froth kept coming out of my mouth. He of course suggested I should swallow it since the doctor thought I was faking it. Fifteen days after I had been discharged from the hospital, I choked over some water and could not even swallow my saliva. My brother contacted the gynaecologist who had done my hysterectomy since my problem had started immediately after the operation."

"It was a Sunday night. We had no medical help but the gynaecologist refused to admit me in his nursing home even for a night and instructed his staff not to answer the phone. He said my problem did not concern them and that night my neighbours and family sat by my bedside, praying and helping me pass the most difficult night of my life. We contacted other doctors, but nobody was willing to take the case and touch me since it was a post-operative problem."

"The following morning, our family doctor shifted me to a private nursing home for observation, where I stayed for four days. They pumped antibiotics through saline but it was not a case of infection. On the fifth day my body started burning from head to toe but there was no rise in my body temperature. I pleaded with the doctor that my body was virtually on fire; he laughed and said that he would call the fire brigade to extinguish the burning feeling. This upset my family and they created a scene. The doctor and staff were prompted to take some action and immediately I was given an IV at a fast flow to remove the heat from my body. An endoscopy was done. It showed that my oesophagus was completely closed. Since the nursing home was not well equipped to treat my kind of case, they were in a hurry to shift me to a bigger hospital. They did not even wait for an ambulance. I was dumped into a taxi."

"The staff of this new hospital left me lying untreated for four hours after which a drip was given by an assistant and I was informed that the gastroenterologist would see me the following day. Then they started a round of dilatation which is extremely painful, uncomfortable and distressing when conducted on a patient who is still conscious. After the second dilatation I asked the doctor what was wrong with me. But the doctor said: "You tell me what is wrong with you. What poison have you taken? Because you have multiple strictures and that can only happen if you have swallowed some acid." I was aghast and furious and told him that. "If I want to die I'd get it right the first time and not allow myself to be tortured like this," I retorted. After one-and-a-half-month's stay in this new hospital and after undergoing eight dilatations and feeling nowhere near better, I decided to return home. By this time I had lost 22 kilograms."

"By January 1994, I was again subjected to dilatations but this time at a municipal hospital where each cost ₹200 instead of the ₹3000 at private hospitals. Here I found the doctors more gentle, caring and humane. The doctors were very optimistic and said that worse cases had improved. Each dilatation was followed by a con-ray-swallow X-ray to check that there was no leak in the oesophagus. I was taking dilatations regularly when one day in May 1994 I met Kashmira Elavia, a spiritual medium and healer, through a common friend. Meeting her was the best thing in my life as through her and her spiritual Guides and through her automatic writing, a bright new universe of Hope and Love entered my life. My old way of thinking peeled off like old, dry, unwanted skin and a new beautiful positive and strong faith and belief began to penetrate my very soul."

"Our Guides promised me love, care and protection. They warned me against dilatation but my family of course opposed it and suggested I do both therapies; dilatation as well as spiritual healing. Little did I realise at that time the strength of the healing power of the spirit world. I realised that when Heaven wills one way mankind can only gaze and wonder. I would go for my dilatation and just when my turn would arrive, the machine would breakdown. At other times the X-ray machine would not be functioning or the doctor would make me wait for hours and send me back home without doing the dilatation."

"Eventually after the fifteenth dilatation, the doctor put her hands up and said that she could not do anything more for me. I was advised to go in for surgery to remove the food pipe and replace it by the colon. I was in tears and ran to Kashmira who just laughed and said, "They told you to stop and you didn't listen, so they had to stop it for you." From then onwards I went to Kashmira for spiritual healing every day for three years. I had stopped all medical treatment completely. I was able to take a diet of strained liquids only. The white froth had stopped coming at such frequent intervals."

"One night during the three-year healing period I dreamt I was standing in a crowd waiting for Sai Baba's darshan. Suddenly a fakir in a white garb pushed everyone and came towards me. He stood and stared at me without talking, then turned away in the opposite direction. I followed him as if mesmerised. He entered a pitch dark basement. I was scared. He knelt down in front of a small Sai Baba murti from which bright beautiful colours glowed. The fakir took the crown and shawl from the murti, wore it and transformed into Sai Baba of Shirdi. I ran, touched His feet and begged Him to heal me. He smiled, applied something on my throat and disappeared. After that I kept seeing Sai Baba in different forms in my dreams for two or three days. I was bewildered. Prior to this, I must state that I was not a Sai Baba devotee. I went to Kashmira to ask her the meaning of these dreams. Through her writing I was informed that Sai Baba was taking care of me and was healing me and since then I have felt a presence at night healing me. I knew it was Sai Baba healing me."

"One day, I met Vira Kheshvala, a friend whom I have known since my childhood days. She came to know about my health and was very upset. She was in regular communication with Meher Baba through her meditation. I asked her permission to attend her meeting. At one of the meetings in 1995, my throat got blocked again and Vira instructed me to put my hand on my throat. Through my hand, I felt a very large hand enveloping my throat with a tingling sensation and that night my throat opened up. I know the hand was that of Meher Baba."

"In August 1995, I was asked to visit a Sai Baba mandir, where many sick people were getting cured. We went on a wrong day and had to return. My office colleague suggested that I should consult a certain doctor at the Tata Memorial Hospital. After a four-hour wait, the doctor just flipped through the reports and did not show much interest. I felt very dejected. Kashmira did not know about my trips to Sai Baba's mandir or to the Tata Memorial Hospital. When I visited her after a gap of almost a month, there was another person waiting to communicate with the spirit world through Kashmira. Instead a message came for me from Sai Baba: *"Meri beti, mujhe idhar-udhar kyon dhundti firti hai? Main tujhe kya udhar mila? Main to tere saath hi hoon. Tujhe kahin bhi janeki zazroorat nahi hai doctor ke pass gayi thi, usne tujhe haath bhi lagaya? Main jo hun, koi bhi doctor tujhe haath nahi laga sakta hai-Main kuch bhi hone nahi dunga."* (My child, why are you going here and there in search of me? Did I meet you there? I am with you all the time. You do not have to search for me in temples. You went to see that doctor. Did he even touch you? I will not allow any doctor to even touch you because I will cure you. When we can put life into a dead body what is your illness? But I cannot come between God and your karma. I can help you to bear it and pray for you. I cannot work out your karma. Have patience and you will be all right). Sai Baba gave me a mantra to chant 108 times daily."

"But stubborn human that I was, I still did not put my full faith in Sai Baba and Meher Baba. In September '96 my throat got choked again for seven days but I didn't tell anyone for four days. I was able to carry on my work as usual. But on the fifth day I started feeling giddy and the next day I was on the verge of collapse as I was unable to take anything all those days. I was given a drip at home for two days. My friend Vira Keshvala prayed to Meher Baba for help. The message that she received said that I should fill a glass with ice cubes and drink that chilled melted water slowly. I did as I was told. I kept on drinking and vomiting and gradually my food pipe opened up. I thought I'd try one more attempt at the operation."

"One of the most prominent surgeons in Bombay whom I consulted emphasised that he could not guarantee success because my case was a very rare one. I wanted to eat solid food and live life like a normal human being so I was willing to go through any amount of discomfort. Another doctor whom I consulted at the Tata Memorial Hospital said I had 70 percent chances of success. So I jumped at the opportunity. Kashmira suddenly got a message without my asking from Sai Baba that I should not undergo this operation since my life was in danger. But I still didn't listen. That is when I learnt my hardest lesson about the will of the Spirit world and the power they hold over our lives."

"In April '97 I underwent all the tests that I was asked to undergo but no beds were available for one entire month. The date was finally set for May 26, 1997. I was admitted one day earlier. My colon was cleansed, several injections were given. A day before the operation, 5 cc of blood was needed for tissue matching. But try as hard as they could, the nurses could not extract a drop of blood from my arms. Finally three nurses and one house-man pressed hard and were barely able to extract three drops of blood from my groin. To this extent my healing Guardian Angels were trying to prevent my surgery. My family, friends and mediums, all were praying hard for the success of this major 10 hour operation."

"The day of the operation dawned bright and clear. I was wheeled into the theatre. Three big circles were attached to my back. Wires were clipped to my fingers and the gas mask was put on my face, but the anaesthetist just could not be traced. My doctor who was dressed in his operation gown with a mask on his face; examining my X rays, suddenly turned to me and inquired 'Are you scared?' When I said no I was not, he replied, 'I am. It is a 10-hour operation but you know what, when I see your stomach, hands and face, I feel that in spite of everything there is something that is taking care of you. In spite of not taking a normal diet your body still looks very healthy which itself is a miracle of sorts. But you know what the most surprising thing is? A sort of message seems to be throbbing in my mind which says not to cut you up. It says don't cut her up. I seem to have forgotten your case history."

"Hearing this I was shocked and stunned. I realised at once that finally Sai Baba was taking the whole matter in His hands. I asked the doctor whether he was postponing the operation because he had someone else to operate upon. But he said, 'No, please believe me when I left my house, sat in the car and came here, I had no idea that I will not be operating on you; but seeing you on the operating table now I just can't think straight. A message keeps on going across my mind and it is so strong that I cannot ignore it. I am not after money. I am not a knife happy doctor to cut you up. I am sorry.' I was then wheeled out of the operation theatre. I could see bewilderment on the faces of those who were assisting him in the operation theatre, because he is an excellent doctor, very well known for his kindness, gentleness and humanitarian qualities as well as medical success in India and abroad."

"Everybody was shocked but happy. A spiritual message was given after a few days that the doctor believed in such paranormal happenings and so it was easy for my

Guardian Angels to communicate with him and thus stop the operation."

"Since May 1997, my throat has not got blocked. I have also regained all the weight I had lost, as now I am able to take a soft diet. I have completely surrendered myself to the spirit world and to my Sai Baba and Meher Baba. I now firmly believe that everybody has some force caring for each one of us. On the other side there are spirits of different degrees of spiritual advancement who take care of us all in this physical plane. Their love and care is miraculous and ultimate and more effective compared to all the doctors and medicines in the world. I suggest to the scornful critics of the spiritual world to open the windows and doors of their minds and experience the divine breeze themselves."

"Ever since my illness five years ago, Meher Baba has been my constant companion. In the past, if I had any doubts about that, He has proved me wrong several times. He has not only protected me, but has also extended His protection towards my son and other members of my family."

"In 1996, one night I dreamt that while returning from school, my son fell into a deep trench dug up on a road. I saw him disappearing down below. I got up with a start, perspiring and trembling all over, because in reality too the roads of our city were dug up and in very bad shape. In fact, just outside his school itself the roads were dug up and left open. I realised that this nightmare was a premonition of some danger about to occur and I was being warned about it. I narrated the dream to my son and prayed fervently to Meher Baba to protect and take care of him. I kept praying to Meher Baba that if the nightmare were to come true ever, He would have to be present and save my son."

"Months passed by and I began to breathe easy. I put aside the nightmare as a figment of my imagination and forgot about it. Two years later, on returning home I noticed my son's hands, arms and legs badly bruised and lacerated. They were cut and bleeding. He then informed me that the lid on the gutter in the garden had given way and he had fallen inside the gutter. I ran down and at the sight of the gutter, I felt as though the blood froze in my body. The lid had broken into two pieces and one bigger part had fallen slantwise, thus breaking his fall and preventing him from going deep down. His cricket bat had fallen so deep that it was not possible to recover it. It was a Sunday evening and usually no one is present in our building at such an hour. Even if there were tenants and he had shouted for help nobody would have heard him as the gutter is in an isolate area. A search conducted for my son would have proved futile as the last place anyone or even I would have imagined to search for would be in the garden and the gutter."

"Even my son was shaken up. He kept repeating that if one of the two broken pieces had not fallen slantwise he would surely have fallen into the deep gutter where even if he would have survived the fall, it would have been impossible for him to get out on his own. He also insisted that he felt someone physically pushing him out of the gutter as he was too scared to do anything on his own and also was way gone down to have been able to help himself out."

"The nightmare had come true, though two years later. I went home straight to Meher Baba's photograph and thanked Him profusely for remembering my plea to Him spoken two years earlier; to be present and save my son if the nightmare should manifest itself in reality. He had as usual kept His promise.

"I sincerely believe that Meher Baba takes care of those who really leave their lives completely in His benevolent hands. My son was appearing for his matriculation examination in May 1997. It was his fifth paper. I was at work. About half-an-hour before his examination, I suddenly began to feel extremely uneasy. It was a busy day at the Bank where I work and there were at least 15 to 20 customers waiting for me to hand them their cash. As a rule – which I always follow no matter what – I never get up from my seat till each and every customer is attended to. It is a rule I follow religiously. But that day it was as though somebody pulled me up from my armpits, made me stand up and literally push me towards the telephone. Finding myself in front of the phone, I remembered my son and rang him up to inquire if all was well. The moment he heard my voice he screamed, "Oh thank God you rang up mummy! Since the last half-an-hour I am trying to ring you up but just cannot get through. How did you know that I was calling out to you? I cannot find my Hall ticket and without it I will not be able to enter the examination room and sit for my exams."

"I took permission from my seniors and just dashed off, praying to Meher Baba to help me. The first miracle was that an empty taxi was parked outside the gate as though waiting for me. We never get a taxi there easily and have to wait for a long time. I picked up my son and went to the examination hall. Usually, you are not let through by the watchman without the ticket but that day he just seemed to smile and hoped that the examiner would allow my son to sit for the exam. Saying Meher Baba's name once again, I approached the examiner and voiced our problem. To my relief he smiled and assured me not to worry. He assured that he would take care of my son and make certain that he sat for the paper. I thanked him profusely and sat in the cab thanking my Meher Baba."

"It was then that I remembered that I had left ₹3,00,000 (Rupees three lakh) in my drawer. In my hurry I had not even bothered to lock it. Three lakh rupees is a huge amount. If it was found missing I would have to compensate the bank and such an amount I could not even dream of possessing. My hands and feet went cold with panic. All the way I prayed to Meher Baba to take care of the money, as many times I have met bank employees of other banks recount tales of how they had to pay through the noses whenever money went missing. On reaching my office, I saw that two of my colleagues had taken charge of my counter, made payments and tallied the cash. There was not a single rupee missing."

"This is the amazing grace of Meher Baba. He takes care of everything; every little detail. Now my entire life is in the hands of God and my Guardian Angels, Meher Baba and Sai Baba.

"JAI BABA"

We spoke for a few more minutes and I left, very humbled and with a feeling of immense security and belonging. We all belonged to God. The only problem was that He still remembered but we had forgotten that we were one big family.

I reached home and my daughter informed that a friend was on the line. I picked up the phone and inquired.

"Hello…"

"Where are you man?"

"One, two, treeee, flour…"

"Pashaan, put the damn receiver down…"

"Daddy I no, I uh…"

"Pashaan vamoose…"

"Daddy is calling me mongoose…"

"Where the hell are you?"

"You know I am trying to write a book on…"

"The Best Way to Drive People Crazy…it sure shall be a best-seller."

"Very funny, By the way I have good news for you…"

"You are leaving India?"

"No. I have just come to know that fatal illnesses can be cured. So now we can take you to the psychic healer to heal your damn brains."

We spoke such encouraging words and then disconnected. I lit a cigarette and looked at the deep blue sky pregnant with puffs of white creamy clouds. Yes, God was in Heaven and everything was well with the world…worlds…all of them, I concluded.

I once again met Vira Kheshvala in early August. It was a Tuesday and messages on the planchette as well as through automatic writing insisted that I complete the book as soon as possible. To make certain that I devoted all my time and energy to the book, evolved folks in Heaven made sure that I did not get involved in any time-consuming affairs, namely full time employment. Jobs would stroll by invitingly. Interviews would be conducted successfully. I would be told to commence work on a particular date. Then heaven would get into the act. A few days before the due date of commencing work, I would be sheepishly informed by my would-be-publishers that they had changed their minds. A week later I would find out that novices were being given permanent jobs, folk whom I had trained were drawing lucrative packets, but Ruzbeh Nari Bharucha remained unemployed…for some evolved folk in heaven with great sense of humour wanted him full-time on their project. (The day I completed writing the book I got a lucrative offer and days later was once again made the executive editor for the very same publishing house for which I had earlier worked).

But let me make one thing very clear. They may have made certain that I remained free and focused on the book, but they never left me in a financial crisis. I had two assignments which made certain that we lived modestly. Yeah, a few notches above the ubiquitous poverty line but we were taken care of and for that I shall be forever indebted. I know that my wife was going through her own crisis which she tried her best not to voice. To see her husband who once was extremely successful now barely able to keep body and soul together was frustrating.

So on a Tuesday afternoon we waited for Meher Castillino. Vira and I spoke about a number of things that day. She had been receiving messages that I was going abroad soon. These messages were received a number of times and thus Vira too was keen that we wrap up the book fast.

"It seems the book will do very well in America. Meher Baba is keen that it gets over fast as they want to let as many people read it before disaster strikes them."

For a while I thought Vira meant before I went to the land of Nike and Coke.

"I did not mean you. I meant disaster in the manner of earthquakes and other natural disasters. Baba as well as Ciam, both have mentioned many times and that too since many years, that from 1997-98 to around 2002 or 2003 the world will go through innumerable natural calamities and more than 60 to 70 per cent of the population shall be wiped out. Earthquakes, floods etc will be rampant."

"Yesterday I was reading about out-of-body experiences. Have you had any of them?"

"Haven't I told you about them?"

"You will be surprised how little anybody has told me about their personal experiences."

"Frankly son, I am so busy with my tailoring assignments that I do not remember. Anyway, the first time I had an out-of-body experience was about four years after Cheherazade and Ketu passed away. I was reading Lobhsang Rampa's book on how to have out-of-body experiences. One afternoon I was very tired and quite frustrated that I was not able to get myself out of my body. By then all my doubts and prejudices had vanished. Ciam, Guru Nanak had also begun communicating with me, and thus I had begun to get confidence. That afternoon I fell asleep but in a short while I felt as though I was floating. I opened my eyes and I saw my body lying on the bed but I was many feet above. I realised that I was experiencing an out-of-body sensation. Someone was guiding me and my astral body floated while I slept soundly on the bed. I kept moving upwards, towards the ceiling and to my horror I saw lots of dust on top of the cupboard. Even in such a state, my first thought was: I am going to tell my servant to clean the top of all the cupboards. I even flicked the dirt but then realised that I was in the astral form and thus my fingers passed through the dust. Then slowly I felt someone guide me back into my body and I woke up immediately. It was not a dream mind you. It really was an out-of-body experience. And yes, there was a lot of dust on top of the cupboard."

"A few months before my husband died, we both were taking a nap in the afternoon, when I saw my husband's astral body float a few inches above his normal body. It was red in colour, very unnaturally red. Those days I did not know the meaning of colours of the astral body. It was later that I learnt that when the astral body became pinkish red it meant death was approaching. I had talked to Phiroze about it but he had not warned me about the approaching disaster. Ten days after my husband died in 1981, once again one afternoon I was lying on my bed, flat on my back, naturally depressed. I was frightened as to how I would cope with life. I was still young, just 46 and had three daughters to take care of. My youngest, Shiraz was only 12. It was then that I left my body and began to hear resounding chants of Om. It was as though a thousand sadhus or monks were praying and chanting the word in unison. It was such a lovely experience that I did not want to enter my body. It was soothing and made me feel so much better and I knew that all would go well."

"Then in 1995-96, I broke my arm and had to be operated upon. Anaesthesia was given and I went to sleep. In seconds, I had my third out-of-body experience. I saw myself sleeping and the doctors operating on me. Then all of a sudden I saw this bright shaft of light and saw my husband smiling at me. Then another shaft of light and in that stood my sister-in-law, Roshan, a very spiritually advanced soul. Both were laughing and smiling at me. I wanted to meet all my dear ones who had passed over but they kept smiling at me. So I angrily asked them to rush and get Cheherazade, Ketu and all my family members."

"Then all of a sudden a brilliant light shone once again and in the shaft stood Dastoorji Kukadaru Saheb, one of the most revered priests in the Zoroastrian religion worshipped by every Zoroastrian. You will find Dastoorji Kukadaru Saheb's photograph in every Parsi house. Kukadaru Saheb then told me that all my problems would be solved. You see all this while I was undergoing a major family problem. I recall that He told me that 'the cause of the problem will migrate soon'. Suddenly they disappeared and I found myself in the body. Everybody thought I was hallucinating when I told them that the cause of the problem will migrate and all will be well."

"Did the person migrate?"

"Yes, but two years later. Remember, when they say soon, it may be in their time span. Basically it is a reassurance that with patience, all will go as planned. The last time I had an out-of-body experience was in Phiroze Kapadia's class. It was a very important day. Lord Buddha's birthday, Purnima. I think it takes place sometime in April-May. I knew from many people that this day was very special as on this day in some remote parts of the Himalayas, the Gurus from the White Brotherhood descend. White Brotherhood is a group of Perfect Masters. Thus Zarathustra, Jesus Christ, Sai Baba, Meher Baba, Guru Nanak and every Saint that has walked the earth is in the White Brotherhood. Only very few souls who are ready are taken by their Gurus. I think it does not matter if you are on the physical plane or astral, the soul should be developed enough and the desire should be strong. They bless the earth, the Indian soil, which is known as the Land of Sages. That day was a Saturday and I was seated in the inner circle. I wanted to know if all this was true and if so, I wanted desperately to see what was going on."

"On that day, for the first time, I fell into a trance. I saw Cheherazade and my sister-in-law Roshan. They smiled and said, "Cooperate with your Guru. He will take you to a beautiful place." All of a sudden I saw myself go out of my body and then found myself standing near thousands of sadhus. They all were in saffron clothes, walking in our direction. I saw Buddha in silver light. He was very huge; say around 10 feet or more, bathed in silver light, in a beautiful robe. I could not see the robe but knew that a robe was there. It had no colour that I could recognise. Then I saw Zarathustra in golden light. Beautiful golden light and He kept beckoning me to follow Him. Cheherazade and Roshan who were standing by my side kept on insisting that I follow Zarathustra. He kept walking ahead and beckoned me to follow, but I just could not follow. Maybe I was scared that I would not be able to return to my body. But it was a beautiful feeling. Then all of a sudden the vision died and I felt myself within my body but I could not get out of the trance. Fortunately for me our Phiroze…he was some powerful medium…Phiroze Kapadia, he helped me out of the trance by slowly praying for me. When I came out of the trance I exhaled with force, as though I had come out of water after a long time. Then I began to cry loudly and once again I went into a trance. He would get me out and I would go back in. After a long time finally he succeeded in making certain that I did not go back into a trance. He then explained that the out-of-body sensation was so beautiful that one does not want to come back to the physical plane; that is why I kept going into a trance and when out of it I would cry and then return."

"While going through the diaries which recorded a few earlier sessions, I came across one dated March 30, 1983; in

Guru Nanak's words on Budh Purnima: 'It is as though the heavens have descended. It is beyond description. Flowers which you all have not imagined, light which the naked eyes cannot behold. Vibrations which would make you shudder in your toes. (Someone inquired whether this took place in the astral world). No my child, in the Himalayas. We come to bless the oldest earth created by God (Is India the oldest? One of them again inquired.) We can descend only on this day, as millions offer prayers and the atmosphere is suitable for us all.'…"

I wondered how it felt to be pronounced medically dead and then, to prove science and technology wrong, wake up and say boo to the medical staff. Near-death experiences are no longer a rarity. So when I reached home at night, I browsed about and within a few days had a clearer idea about near-death experiences. It seems that these occurrences are now being experienced by a greater number of people, maybe because the need to be comforted and warned about life existing after death has never been greater.

Nearly two decades ago, a survey conducted in America revealed that virtually eight million people or one in 20, had experienced at least one near-death experience. Near-death experiences have been reported in books written centuries earlier, from Plato to Tolstoy to Jung. A famous narrative of a near-death experience by Monk Bede, an extremely respected English historian is given below.

> There was a head of a family living in a place in the country of the Northumbrians, known as Cunningham, who led a devout life with all his household. He fell ill and grew steadily worse until the crisis came, and in the early hours of one night he died. But at daybreak he returned to life and suddenly sat up to the great consternation of those weeping around the body, who ran away; only his wife, who loved him more dearly, remained with him,

though trembling and fearful. The man reassured her and said: "Do not be frightened; for I have truly risen from the grasp of death and I am allowed to live among men again. But henceforth I must not live as I used to and must adopt a very different way of life"...Not long afterward, he abandoned all worldly responsibilities and entered the monastery of Melrose....

Then the good man, who had virtually risen from the dead and nearly killed a large section of family and friends with terror of the unknown, narrated what he had seen and experienced.

A handsome man in a shining robe was my guide, and we walked in silence in what appeared to be a north-easterly direction. As we travelled onward, we came to a very broad and deep valley of infinite length...He soon brought me out of darkness into an atmosphere of clear light, and as he led me forward in bright light, I saw before us a tremendous wall which seemed to be of infinite length and height in all directions. As I could see no gate, window, or entrance in it, I began to wonder why we went up to the wall. But when we reached it, all at once – I know not by what means – we were on top of it. Within lay a very broad and pleasant meadow... Such was the light flooding all this place that it seemed greater than the brightness of daylight or of the sun's rays at noon...

(The guide said)..."You must now return to your body and live among men once more; but, if you will weigh your actions with greater care and study to keep your words and ways virtuous and simple, then when you die, you too will win a home among these happy spirits that you see. For, when I left you for a while, I did so in order to discover what your future would be."

When he told me this, I was most reluctant to return to my body; for I was entranced by the pleasantness and beauty of the place I could see and the company I saw there. But I did not dare to question my guide, and meanwhile, I know not how, I suddenly found myself alive among men once more.

One of the most amazing books on death and the life after is *The Tibetan Book Of Living And Dying* by Sogyal Rinpoche, born in Tibet, who entered the monastic life when he was just six months old. Sogyal Rinpoche is the incarnation of Tertön Sogyal, a renowned mystic, virtually a self-made master and a mentor of the Thirteenth Dalai Lama; an amazing book written by an authority. The book is a serious study of life after death and the philosophy is simple: by learning about death, we learn how to live. The entire book is a treasure house. I have taken the above extract as well as all the accounts of near-death experiences from this book. Apart from being a storehouse of information, *The Tibetan Book Of Living And Dying* has a number of references and extracts from other well-known books dealing with paranormal phenomena. Below are extracts from *The Tibetan Book Of Living And Dying*, in reality they are extracts from various other books dealing with near-death experiences, quoted by the Rinpoche:

"One of the main features of the near-death experience is the impression of moving at terrific speed and feeling weightless through a black space, a total, peaceful, wonderful blackness, and down a long, dark, tunnel. One woman told Kenneth Ring, (the author of Heading Towards Omega: In Search Of The Meaning Of The Near-Death Experience): It's just like a void, a nothing and it's such a peaceful it's so pleasant that you can keep going. It's a complete blackness, there is no sensation at all, and there was no feeling sort of like a dark tunnel, just a floating. It's like being in mid-air.

"*Another woman told him (Kenneth Ring, the author of Heading Towards Omega: In Search Of The Meaning Of The Near-Death Experience): The first thing I remember was a tremendous rushing sound, a tremendous…it's hard to find the right words to describe. The closet thing that I could associate it with is, possibly, the sound of a tornado – a tremendous gushing wind, but almost pulling me. And I was being pulled into a narrow point from a wide area.*"

"*A woman told Margot Grey (author of Return From Death: An Experience of the Near-Death Experience): I was in what felt like outer space. It was absolutely black out there and I felt like I was being drawn towards an opening at the end of a tunnel. I knew this because I could see a light at the end; that's how I knew it was there. I was vertical and I was being drawn towards the opening. I know it wasn't a dream; dreams don't happen that way. I never once imagined it was a dream.*

"*Melvin Morse, (author of Closer to the light: Learning from Children's Near-Death Experience), who has specialised in the research of near-death experience in children, remarks: 'Nearly every near-death experience of children (and about one-fourth of those of adults) has in it an element of light. They all report that the light appears at the final stages of the near-death experience, after they have had an out-of-body experience or have traveled up the tunnel.*"

"*One of the best descriptions of the approach to light was reported by Margot Grey: Then gradually you realize that way, far off in the distance, an immeasurable distance, you may be reaching the end of the tunnel, as you can see a white light, but it's so far away I can only compare it to looking up into the sky and in the distance seeing* a single star, but visually you must remember that you are looking through a tunnel and this light would fill the end of the tunnel. You concentrate on the speck of light because as you are propelled forward, you anticipate reaching this light."

"Gradually, as you travel towards it at an extreme speed it gets larger and larger. The whole process on reflection only seems to take about one minute. As you gradually draw nearer to this extremely brilliant light, there is no sensation of an abrupt end of the tunnel, but rather more of a merging into the light. By now the tunnel is behind you and before you is this magnificent, beautiful blue-white light. The brilliance is so great, brighter than a light that would immediately blind you, but absolutely does not hurt your eyes at all."

"One of the best descriptions of not just seeing a bright light but the type of light is given by many of those who have been through the near-death experience. My description of the light was-well, it was not a light, but the absence of darkness, total and complete...Well, you think of light as a big light shining on things making shadows and so forth. This light was really the absence of darkness. We're so used to that concept because we always get a shadow from the light unless the light is all around us. But this light was so total and complete that you didn't look at the light, you were in the light."

"Another description of light by Kenneth Ring (the author of Heading Towards Omega: In Search Of The Meaning Of The Near-Death Experience): It was not bright. It was like a shaded lamp or something. But it wasn't that kind of light you get from a lamp. You know what it was? Like someone had put a shade over the sun. It made me feel very, very peaceful. I was no longer afraid. Everything was going to be all right. And yet another description: *The light is brighter than anything you could possibly imagine. There are no words to describe it. I was so happy, it's impossible to explain. It was such a feeling of serenity, it was a marvelous feeling. The light is so bright that it would normally blind you, but it doesn't hurt one's eyes a bit."*

"A number of those who have described light have mentioned the feeling of oneness with the light. I had no separate identity. I was the light and one with it. Another explanation to Margot Grey: *Only my essence was felt. Time no longer mattered and space was filled with bliss. I was bathed in radiant light and immersed in the aura of the rainbow. All was fusion. Sounds were of a new order, harmonious, nameless.* Another detailed explanation once again of Margot Grey goes thus: *The following series of events appear to happen simultaneously, but in describing them I will have to take them one at a time. The sensation is of a being of some kind, more a kind of energy, not a character in the sense of another person, but an intelligence with whom it is possible to communicate. Also, in size it just covers the entire vista before you. It totally engulfs everything, you feel enveloped. The light immediately communicates with you, in an instant telekinesis your thought waves are read, regardless of language. A doubtful statement would be impossible to receive. The first message I received was 'Relax, everything is beautiful, everything is OK, you have nothing to fear.' I was immediately put at absolute ease. In the past if someone, like a doctor had said 'It is OK, you have nothing to fear, this will not hurt', it usually did – you couldn't trust them. But this was the*

*most beautiful feeling I have ever known, it's absolute
pure love. Every feeling, every emotion is just perfect.
You feel warm, it has nothing to do with temperature.
Everything is absolutely vivid and clear. What the light
communicates to you is a feeling of true, pure love. You
experience this for the first time ever. You can't compare
it to the love of your wife, or the love of your children or
sexual love. Even if all those things were combined, you
cannot compare it to the feeling you get from this light."*

If you are wondering how come each one experiences different emotions and sensations, according to me there may be two answers. The first could be that each spirit experiences a slight difference because they may be recounting the plane, stage, phase or world etc to which their soul moved initially but then returned to the physical plane. Each soul has its own baggage and thus moves towards a different level of consciousness and dimension. This could be one explanation. The other could be that the descriptive powers and the power to absorb fine vibrations differ from people to people. Not all love Chopin. My entire family would be snoring loud and clear 15 minutes into the musical serenade while there are many Chopin lovers who experience a high and really feel uplifted and refreshed.

Another man who had nearly drowned while still a kid recounts to Melvin Morse: *"As I reached the source of the Light, I could see in. I cannot begin to describe in human terms the feelings I had over what I saw. It was a giant infinite world of calm, and love, and energy, and beauty. It was as though human life was unimportant compared to this. And yet it urged the importance of life at the same time as it solicited death as a means to a different and better life. It was all being, all beauty, all meaning for all existence. It was all the energy of the universe forever in one place."*

Another lovely account of how clairvoyant abilities seem all of a sudden to be possessed by the spirit of the person experiencing near-death is vividly told to *Raymond Moody Jr, the author of Life After Life*. *"...All of a sudden, all knowledge of all that had started from the very beginning, that would go on without end – for a second I knew all the secrets of the ages, all the meaning of the universe, the stars, the moon – of everything. There was a moment in this thing – well there isn't any way to describe it – but it was like I knew all things... for a moment, there, it was like communication wasn't necessary. I thought whatever I wanted to know could be known. While I was there I felt at the center of things. I felt enlightened and cleansed. I felt I could see the point of everything. Everything fitted in, it all made sense, even the dark times. It almost seemed, too, as if the pieces of a jigsaw all fitted together."*

Of course, not all near-death experiences are pleasant and brimmed with heavenly emotion. "Some people report terrifying experiences of fear, panic, loneliness, desolation and gloom...one person reported by Margot Grey spoke of being sucked into 'a vast black vortex like a whirlpool' and those who have negative experiences tend to feel, rather like those about to be reborn in lower realms... that they are travelling downward instead of upward. One recounted to Margot Grey the following:

> *"I was moving along as part of a river of sound – a constant babble of human noise... I felt myself sinking into and becoming part of the stream and slowly being submerged by it. A great fear possessed me as if I knew that once overcome by this ever growing mass of noise I would be lost. I was looking down into a large pit, which was full of swirling gray mist and there were all these hands and arms reaching up and trying to grab hold of me and drag me in there. There was a terrible wailing noise, full of desperation."*

Many have experienced extreme discomfort either of

unimaginable cold or intense and unbearable heat or sounds of wailing and chaos.

> *"A woman reported to Margot Grey: I found myself in a place surrounded by mist. I felt I was in hell. There was a big pit with vapor coming out and there were arms and hands coming out trying to grab mine... I was terrified that these hands were going to claw hold of me and pull me into the pit with them... An enormous lion bounded towards me from the other side and I let out a scream. I was not afraid of the lion, but I felt somehow he would unsettle me and push me into that dreadful pit... It was very hot down there and the vapor or steam was very hot."*

"Raymond Moody, Jr, (the author of *Life After Life*) writes that several people claimed to have seen beings who seemed trapped by their inability to surrender their attachments to the physical world: possessions, people or habits. One woman spoke of these 'bewildered people': *What you would think of as their head was bent downward, they had sad depressed looks; they seemed to shuffle, as someone would on a chain gang... they looked washed out, dull, gray. And they seemed to be forever shuffling and moving around, not knowing where they were going, not knowing who to follow, or what to look for. As I went by they didn't even raise their heads to see what was happening. They seemed to be thinking, 'Well, it's all over with. What am I doing? What's it all about?' Just this absolute, crushed, hopeless demeanour — not knowing what to do or where to go or who they were or anything else. They seemed to be forever moving, rather than just sitting, but in no special direction. They would start straight, then veer to the left and take a few steps and veer back to the right. And absolutely nothing to do. Searching, but for what they were searching I don't know."*

The more I get involved with this subject the more I get

amazed by my own ignorance and that of our generation that sees no virtue, hears no virtue, talks no virtue except the virtue that is directly related to a financial reward. Put the bucks on the table and God and Heaven can be relegated to the confines of a dusty cupboard, or in one of the library's least used corners. It really astounds me that starting from the blazing sun that shines on us and makes us believe that it revolves when in reality it is us who do the spinning about continuously; the same way it is with God and the spirit world and our sense of priorities. The spirit world is the final reality but we in our amazing need to rush hither and thither assume that the spirit world is an illusion of unemployed editors and poets and yogis who go about putting themselves in various knots and twists to just pass time. What seems to be real is hard cash. What one should firmly keep in mind is that nightfall and darkness occur when that portion of the revolving globe turns its back on the sun. Not because the sun seemingly sets into the ocean. The same way darkness in our lives is caused when we turn our backs to God. Not because God does not care. The poor Pa in heaven in all-keen and ready to help but what can he do when ears are shut, backs are shown and His very real world is shrugged off as an outdated hallucination?

The communication on the planchette was moving slowly, so, as per the advice of Meher Baba, Vira Kheshvala went into a trance and we had two sittings of half-an-hour each. The speed with which Vira Kheshvala spoke necessitated us to record the answers. Thanks once again to Meher Castillino who for some reason unknown even to her, felt forced to carry her rarely used Dictaphone. I know Vira's normal way of speaking to realise the difference in the manner in which she spoke when in a trance. Usually, Vira has a soft, even apologetic voice. She has a self-effacing attitude and does not take herself seriously. Also, normally she speaks more in Gujarati and less in English but in the trance she spoke only in English and the tone was full of confidence. It was a tone of authority yet filled with warmth. I have left the English unchanged, not for any other reason but to show the reader two different levels of communication through which the answers came. I asked the questions and they were voiced by Meher Baba but through Vira; thus, often there came a time when Meher Baba wanted to say something which Vira found hard to pick up and midway, the sentence was altered.

Q) JAI BABA. (It is a manner of offering salutations to Meher Baba and a common way of greeting amongst Meher Baba devotees). What takes place after death?

MB) When the soul goes out of the body, what takes place after death first of all depends on the evolution of the soul. If the soul knows the subject then there won't be any difficulty in transition, otherwise if the soul is ignorant of what he has to expect, then he is made to sleep by his Guides. The Guides come and flock around his bed including his dear ones. They all surround him and one by one they take turns in pacifying the soul. If the soul is ready he will be very (eager), ready to go, otherwise he will fight to come back into the body. Then the work of the Guides begins. They make him understand that the thread of life has snapped and he cannot enter the body any more. He has to go further into the astral world. He is guided if he is not aware of the subject. He is caught hold of like a baby and taken to the astral world, through a tunnel, a dark tunnel. Then he emerges into a light, a brilliant light; that (the intensity of the light) too depends on the progress of the soul. If the progress is slow, the light is dim. If the progress is good, the light is so brilliant that you actually can't see (into it), it's such a brilliant ray of light. Then the soul has to go and if the soul still persists in fighting, then the doctors on our side make him sleep by giving him a sort of sedative, just as your doctors do in your world... (The soul) is made to sleep in the hall of rest. There, Guides monitor him like doctors. He is monitored and in each waking moment of his, the Guide is ready and able to help him. So are his relatives. The relatives are pushed in front of him so he feels comfortable; and the most attached soul which has passed before him, helps him (the new entrant) to visualise the other world. Then slowly the soul gets up (awakens). He is taught like a child by his Guru, his Guide that this is a parallel world where he has to start living now. So the soul goes with the Guide and first he is shown where he will remain, his plane so to say.

There are seven planes, my children and according to the progress of the soul, the Guru is able to show him the class; as if in a school, seventh grade or sixth grade or fifth grade or fourth grade or whatever. He is made to sit under the teacher who is able to take him further in his progress. Then slowly he is taught how to live in this other world. If the soul is very gross then he will think of material things and whatever he thinks will be produced. He will think of a car or diamonds or food (and) everything will be provided to him. Nothing is denied to the soul, the soul has to saturate itself till it says, 'No more my Guides. I know now this is of no use, all is left behind'.

Then the soul is ready to work for his Guides, his Guru and from thence on he is allotted different work. If a person is happy with a natural surrounding like trees and plants and flowers, he is made a gardener to grow beautiful blooms in the garden of God. If he is interested in science and computers… we have computers which no one on earth can copy; no one can even imagine… the vast knowledge that we have here. He is taken to a library first where the *Akashik* record is given. *Akashik* records my children, are records of your whole life, past karmas, past life, several lives, all recorded in the Akashik records. And believe Me when that soul reads (his records) he is so awed by it (and) he is so surprised that he has passed so many lives before that he is not interested in that previous life anymore. He wants to know further what sort of life he is going to face ahead. What sort of life lies ahead of him, he is supposed to live and then on he progresses to different fields.

(The soul) He can do anything that he desires. There is no restriction. A soul can go to a lower plane but he cannot enter a higher plane than the one in which he is (placed). I hope you understand my children. That means a soul cannot stay in a higher plane than that he has progressed to in his life. So we tell you from time to time (to) pray more, progress more and leave out material things. Do not seek material things. Material things are of no value in this other world. Only progress, only see the light, see the light of God. See God in your own image. Go within. Seek God. Seek not wealth my children. But seek the higher truth. God is great.

Q) Meher Baba, how long does a soul stay in a particular plane? Does it depend on the soul and if it doesn't, who decides when the soul will reincarnate? Is reincarnation optional?

MB) No, my child, reincarnation is a must. If you have to progress you have to reincarnate. According to our Zoroastrian religion they say there is no reincarnation but that is not true. The religion, the scripture, is misunderstood, misinterpreted. A soul has to reincarnate and when the soul passes on to the other world (the stay in the spirit world) depends as I told you before, on the material attachment, the phase (the plane) the soul has come into; if the soul has detached (itself) from earth and then moved on, his passing and stay in the astral world will be very easy. Otherwise he will be drawn from time to time to the earth. He will (then) be called an earthbound soul. But he is prevented from going back very fast by his Guru, by his Guides. He is shown the better path of life. This (the spirit world) is your real life. The astral world is your real life. This (physical life on earth) is your living death. In your world, it's your living death. So when the soul goes (arrives in the astral world) he is made to understand that the real life is there with us, with their Guru, with their Masters, with their dear ones who have passed before him. The soul has to stay and progress in the astral world; and it depends again on the training the child has got from the beginning till he passes over, (training) from his parents, from his teachers. Whatever truth the child gathers from your world, he takes it along. His mind continues and so he will opt to stay in the astral world more or less. The final decision is the soul's, but he is guided by his Gurus and he is told that progress is faster in your material world. I am ashamed to say that the soul has to detach from our vibrations and go back to your material wealth, your material wants, your material needs. I am ashamed to say material wants have become so vast, so vast that people don't understand (what they are doing). In the name of power they kill each other. They frame each other. Crime is committed. It is only karmic but sill it is a crime. Karmic or not Karmic, every human being has to progress in your world and the progress is slower in our world. Ultimately he has to reincarnate. He has to go back and he has to start life again. But if he tries earnestly to improve himself, to detach from material wants, from material wealth… just teach your children to say 'thank you God, no more. I am saturated. I am filled to the brim' and then growth will be faster, higher and more progressive.

Q) Meher Baba, what if a soul does not want to move fast but would rather move slowly but surely and steadily in the spirit world? Does the soul yet have to come back? What if the soul says: 'No, I don't mind moving slowly but surely' because the earth is filled with temptations and the soul can go astray. What then?

MB) When the soul reaches that stage my child, then he is almost ready to merge with God. That is the time when he will say… he will refuse to come to earth. So his progress is more. He will progress slowly in our world and he will merge with God, life…he will merge like water merges with milk or milk merges with water. That is what it is. That stage of time the soul can say 'I don't want to go back' and he will be allowed to stay in our world and progress slowly. But by that time the soul must have reached the seventh plane of existence. That is when the soul will say 'I don't what to go back'. But again he (most probably the soul) has to come (back to earth or the physical plane) because he has to guide others below him as a mentor or as head girl or a head boy of a school. He has to look after his flock. He has to steer the lower children up to where he is standing so he has to go (return). He has no choice. But the choice can be slower.

Q) But Meher Baba, can't the soul help his flock by becoming their spiritual guide? Does he have to come down? Because when he comes down there is a possibility that he might go astray, isn't there?

MB) No, my child, by the time you go on a higher plane all your karmic links (desires) have been fulfilled. You have become a beggar. You have become a murderer. You have created crime. You have finished crime. You have done everything. You have flung insults. You have said bad words. You have done bad deeds. All that you have passed, then you have come to a higher level. So you cannot go back. After matriculation you cannot opt to become a child again and go to a nursery class. So it is the same way. You have to progress and then show others the same progress that he (the soul) has made. He in his turn is helping others. So his karma is again linked with the lower souls. His karma is getting fulfilled with the lower souls and the lower souls in their turn when they go higher and higher will have the same cycle. Just as the cycle of birth and rebirth, this is the cycle… the karmic cycle of progress and (more) progress. When you come and touch the feet of your Master that is your highest progress. My child, when you are young and link to your Guru it is your highest progress. So never for one minute think that you are doing something wrong by going into spiritualism. The time has come. The doors of your abode in heaven are open wide. Do not for a moment think that you are doing something wrong. Help others. Help, extend your arms as your mentor would do. Extend your arms to those who are not ready. Extend your arms to those who need them more than you do. Help. Give as much as you can. Give till it pains. Give till your arms stretch out, far and wide. Help and you will get your reward in heaven above.

Q) Meher Baba, I would like to know if the seven stages you have mentioned can be classified into astral worlds and causal worlds, where the causal world is the last stage, the seventh stage? Because a number of books describe them as worlds, astral and causal and others depict the spirit dimension as stages. What is the term which is most appropriate?

MB) Planes my child. (Use the word) planes. There are different worlds. Mental world… causal, astral but you can write (planes)… simplify it. Everybody cannot understand. Simplify it as much as you can. Make it humorous, make it readable, make it very enlightened and make it (use the word) planes.

Q) Meher Baba, you have given them a number of titles, which according to you is the most appropriate?

MB) The titles are given by Ciam (Guru Nanak) not by me. You use your discretion and whatever fits in, you can use. I am sure they will be all very enlightened good names. Ciam is the highest, one of the highest White Brotherhood souls and you all are lucky to have Him as your Guru, as your Guide, as your enlightened spiritual leader. Be thankful, be happy and always say thank you to Him.

Q) Meher Baba, is it true that when somebody expires and his relatives and fiends grieve over the death of that person that it...?

MB) That is ignorance. That is in ignorance. They don't know what they are doing. They are harming the soul, they are luring it back to earth instead of letting it go. Let the soul go my child. Don't cling to anything; least of all to your dear ones. Let them go ahead and in their turn they will help you. Don't try to hold them back. Don't try to cry over them. Crying is the worst thing. They will be drawn towards you. They will be very sad because they cannot show themselves to you. At the same time they can see you do everything. Each moment of your day they are with you. Whenever you need them they are with you. They are allowed to come anytime that you want them to. If you think of them and ask for real help they'll help but not material help. I'm again and again saying not material help, only help to develop and evolve; how to leave this physical garb (which) you have to shed. You have to tear your clothes and leave (materialism) and wear the garb of a king or a queen in the astral world, my child.

Q) Meher Baba, what and who are ghosts? These so-called evil spirits who sometimes harm people, haunt and scare them. What kind…?

MB) They are the lowest form of spirits. They are on the very lowest rung of the ladder. They have not evolved anywhere. They have no prayers. They don't know God, they don't know any Guru; they don't have any guidance and just live from day to day like animals. Even animals are helped my child but not these souls. These souls are on a very low realm of progress. They'll take umpteen years to take birth and rebirth…and then they will progress. After they have reached the third plane they will be ready to seek help from a higher guru. Till then these souls are earthbound. They want to come back into their bodies. They want to take rebirth very fast. They are allowed to take birth and rebirth very fast because they have to progress in your world. In your world, as I said, the progress is faster. So they have to come again and again and again. Their birth and death cycles are very fast. They die young and again they take birth and they take rebirth with a vengeance. They want to finish their karma. Although they want to progress, their advancement his hampered as they are the criminal minded ones. They only think of crime and not of the Guru. Crime according to our standard of thinking is karmic also. So they have to pass through all these phases before they come to the third level and after the third level, fourth level, fifth level and again different phases (each plane has many stages of evolution)…like different standards, they have to pass through many standards and then they come (reach) higher. These lower souls… they need more prayers than they can imagine; and when prayers are not done for them, they have no one to guide them. They have no prophet to reach out to. So these are the lower souls. The ghosts…the so-called ghosts who wander around. They don't know there to go. They can't come to the higher astral world and they can't take birth fast unless they are helped; these are the wandering souls. They take pleasure in disturbing other souls. They take pleasure and pride in giving…misgivings to other higher souls. Thy try to harm them. But actually they need help. So when you feel that some bad shakti (power or spirit) is around you, try to pray (for them). Pray for their souls and say 'whoever you are, please go and rest. You cannot harm me because I am protected by my Guru' and then pray for that soul. These prayers will help. Prayers are your bridge to Heaven. Prayers are a must. Prayers you have to do night and day. Any form of prayer. By way of charity…charity is also your prayer. Good karmas are also your prayers. Pray, pray, pray my children. Meditate, meditate, meditate as much as you can. Day and night just close your eyes and think of Him, Him, Him, Him and Him.

Q) Meher Baba, these so-called un-evolved souls…why are they so un-evolved and why don't they have some kind of Guardian Angel or why don't they have some kind of Prophet to take care of them? Aren't they the creations of God?

MB) I am telling you that these are the souls from the animal kingdom. They are still between the stage of humanity and the animal kingdom. So their Guides and their Gurus are also on a lower plane. Your Gurus and Guides are from the White Brotherhood. Can you understand me? White Brotherhood is the highest form of Masters that co-exists. These are the *Ameshaspands* (Angels) in your language. In your religions they are the right hand of God; and they have better things to do than to help these lower souls. Lower souls have lower guides. Those that have gone from kindergarten to the first class. They will help them. Now can you imagine the knowledge of a first standard child? Can you imagine what he can help and teach a kindergarten child? Same way these souls who have graduated from the animal kingdom have got very low souls as Guides, so they will get guidance on a very low footing; and after several birth (and) rebirth cycles they will start climbing the ladder to God's realm.

Q) How does one make certain that only good spirits stay in one's home and around one's family and friends?

MB) What a silly question, my child. Your prayers, your vibrations are so high that no other soul can penetrate. No lower soul can penetrate ever. Your prayers are so vibrant. They are so powerful that these souls cannot penetrate. They have to seek their own abode. They cannot go on a higher (level)... a lower kindergarten child cannot go to college. Can you understand that? When you feel any bad vibrations around you...you have to bring water from the sea, sprinkle it on your doorstep. Why are you asking Me this question? Have you got anything... any doubt in your house?... then do this my child. Bring water from the ocean...from the sea. Bring it bottled at home. Put it on your prayer table. Pray to it. Make the water very purified with your prayer vibrations. Keep the cork of the bottle open. Better still, put it (the water) in an open glass. Let your vibrations fall on this water. Then sprinkle the water in the evening time (during sunset). Sprinkle the water on the doorstep of your house and burn some loban. (Loban is the resin of a tree with the botanical name of *Styrax Benzoin* and is used in making incense. One can use incense sticks also). Go around your house, use loban, then pray and at the same time sprinkle this holy water from the sea that you have purified. Then there will not be any bad shakti (power or spirit) around. That is all.

Q) Meher Baba, are there other planets like earth where life exists, as we know it?

MB) Yes, higher planets. Very highly evolved souls live on them and a time will come when they too will come and help earth people. Like we do from the astral world. They (the planets) are forms lower than the astral so they will also be able to help earth people when the time comes and the earth is getting ready to get destroyed. Thousand are ready to take part. These other planet people will come and help these souls when they struggle for life. They will be able to help and then they will be taken to the astral world in large masses and the earth will be cleansed of all evil; and the holy people will be able to come down and take care of your earth. For those who have survived the holocaust there will be a beautiful, bright world which is coming very soon now. So my children we are telling you to keep ready so that you don't need so much help. You can help yourself. Let others who are ignorant get help from these evolved planets. You will be able to stand on your own feet. You will be able to guide others to our astral world. That is all. I think my child needs rest.

We sat for the next séance on a wet Monday afternoon. Vira meditated for a few seconds, but first said her *kusti* prayers. Meher and I sat on different stools while Vira sat on the bed, in her usual place of daily meditation.

Q) Jai Baba. Dear Meher Baba, please explain in detail the soul's journey from the time it becomes an individual identity till the time it merges back with God?

MB) When a soul is allotted a womb, it is done through the help of a Guide and Guru both together. The last incarnation's relationships (relations from the last birth) are the Guides and they assimilate his karmic dues (and) with the help of the Guiding light, the soul is allotted a womb. It is up to the soul to select the womb and the final word is the soul's, so when he takes birth he assimilates all his past karmas. He wants to finish as much as he can and he takes on the burden on his shoulder to finish whatever he wants to finish. Then he takes birth and when the dues are too many to fulfil the soul crumbles under his own weight of karmic dues and that is when the soul suffers and through this suffering he again seeks God's help. Then his Guiding light again will help him in turn and this is how the karmic dues are from time to time finished. Through one birth to the other and once the soul's journey is finished he again goes to the astral world. He again assimilates (his karma) when he is given the records... the Akashik records. He is made to read what he has finished and whatever he is not able to finish he has again to take birth and do it (finish his pending karma) in the next incarnation. So that is how this cycle goes on and on till he, the soul reaches the highest rung of the ladder and he is almost ready to merge with God.

Q) Dear Meher Baba, actually what I wanted to inquire was what you had mentioned earlier, that each individual soul has to go through a number of different incarnations in different bodies, through different species of living organisms and even after he incarnates as a man, he has to go through a number of experiences. From a murderer to an evolved man, he has to experience everything, Why?

MB) Because my child he has separated from God's light. He has to again submerge, merge himself with God's light. That is God's play. You cannot understand (but) it's His fiddle. He plays on His violin the music; God's music. Notes you will not understand my child till you merge with Him. Till you see the light, till you hear His music you will not understand. The cycle is His game, his chessboard. (You all are) His actors that play the roles and this is His vast game. The whole universe, the whole vast cosmos is His chessboard where his plays and passes His time. God enjoys each moment of it, each second God is aware. With the help of His helpers, he like a king knows what is happening (and where) and he is connected to all His children. Wherever they are, in whichever place they are, He knows each and every soul's progress. He is 'Mahatma'. He is the ultimate. There is no parallel to His game of chess.

Q) But Meher Baba, why does the soul have to experience such evil deeds. You have mentioned earlier that each soul, each individual has to go through insulting people, robbing, murdering and slowly with each birth progress. Why does the soul have to…?

MB) They are lower souls my child, that take birth from the animal kingdom into human beings, they are gross, they are still in the animal world. Their minds have still not shifted over to the human kingdom. So like animals they take revenge on each other, devour each other. They take… they eat away like cannibals. First the cannibals had started. (The first humans were cannibals). Then gradually came humans (in) better forms. These are the lower souls; they have to gain experience my child. The crimes are the karmic dues that are paid back. Just like animals take revenge on each other, these human beings also take revenge on each other and they opt to finish this in the lower rung of the ladder and the lower stage of evolution. After you reach a certain age, say about when you have reached the third or the fourth plane, all this will eventually get less and less and you will become a better soul, a better evolved person. You won't think of taking revenge. You will start understanding the ways of God and you will start forgiving. 'Forgive and forget' is the motto of your life my child. You have to forgive and forget and take everything that comes in your way as God's seed that you are sowing in your garden of heaven.

Q) Dear Meher Baba, does each individual soul have to pass from the animal to human kingdom? Do all of us have to pass the many stages of evolution?

MB) Animals when they reach the (stage of) cattle, the dog, the cat, the tamed animals (it's a higher stage of evolution from wild animals) then they are ready to go into the human kingdom. There are (lower) planes in the animal kingdom also. So when they reach the stage of a dog or a cat or cattle they have started getting the love of human beings. That is why we say love all animals, my child. Because the animal has to shed its fear. When the fear is shed then he is ready… the animal is ready to take birth in the human kingdom and from the human kingdom they are again on a very lower level. (These new entrants have to finish their so-called evil attributes and do so by taking births and rebirths at a quick pace). Then they reach the third level which is also supposed to be a lower level but then the soul starts to understand his very being. Starts to understand the why of God's working and then the birth cycle is a little slower and he finishes his karma and then he is ready to graduate to the fourth plane and then move upwards.

Q) Dear Meher Baba, if everything is destined, if everything is karma, what is in our hands?

MB) Nothing. Nothing is in your hands; destiny is chalked out. It is God's will. It is his subordinates who plan everything for you. Your whole life, like a story, is planned out for you my child. You are just the actor in God's realm (God's film). It is His film, His drama that you are acting in. You are nowhere. You are nothing, just a plain actor and as an actor has to listen to his director, the same way you have to listen to your Guides, your Gurus, your God. It is His play. His life that you are living. God is playing a game with you my child. There is no say in the matter. You have nothing to do in the life span of a human being. You can change a little bit. From one lane to the other. That is all. From one role to the other, that is all. You don't have to do anything else. You have to abide by your destiny my child. Destiny can be changed by your hands only very, very slowly. You can change it very minutely. You can change it negligibly, otherwise you have to follow what you have taken birth for. Where you have gone wrong, the Gurus will tell you and that is when you can change yourself a little bit. Improve yourself a little bit by prayers, by guidance, by your Guru's thought you can abide by their wishes. Nothing else will change your destiny.

Q) But Meher Baba, so many times people take advantage of this fact. They say nothing is in my hands, so they don't make the effort. They don't try. Don't pray, I mean…

MB) That is also wrong. You have to live a life which is beautiful. Take a rose. When it opens its petals one by one and when you see it blooming, you will admire it. Same way you have to live your life, like a rose my child. Let the scent waft around you and let nature take care of you. You have to take whatever you can in the best way. The best route. You can't go on a hilly road and puncture your tyres. You have a take your diversion in a better way, that is what.

Q) Dear Meher Baba, according to the Hindu *shastras* we have to take birth countless times. So we take birth to experience each and every living creature and then come to the human stage?

MB) I cannot tell you the exact number of times a soul has to be reborn but a human being can take a sort of promotion from school; from the 1st standard he can jump into the 3rd standard. He can jump into the 3rd standard if he has done well in his last life. If he outsmarts the other pupils he can skip one lifetime. A full lifetime can be skipped. If your actions are good, if your thoughts are good. If your love is good for mother nature (then you can skip one entire lifetime); love, love, love, love everybody. Like Mother Teresa, her life was fulfilled completely by loving the lowest, the lowest rung of poor people…she loved them, cared for them. She brought them to her fold and this mother Teresa, this soul, attained sainthood by doing such deeds. By such actions where there is no parallel, where she did not wait for any rewards. It was coming naturally from within. With love from within. Her whole soul, her whole body was encased in love. There was nothing else besides love. She was generating love and that is why we say you can skip so may '*Janams*' (births) and go higher, progress faster.

Q) Dear Meher Baba, why do certain religions tolerate non-vegetarianism and some religions insist on vegetarianism?

MB) These are good attributes we tell you to follow but it's up to each soul to do so. When you, when an animal becomes a human being, the first form of humanity was cannibalism and that has gone from the earth though in some parts, in very remote parts there is still cannibalism. That is the lowest soul. The lowest rung of humanity and then eventually you start shifting from human flesh to animal flesh. The soul has to be satisfied with blood and flesh. Afterwards, after a few evolutions you will shed all that and you will from within start eating…turning into a vegetarian and after you become a vegetarian your aura changes. Your so-called life changes. You admire nature and you will again start thinking that vegetables also have lot of life. Why should we eat vegetables? But you have to survive. You have to eat something. You can't just live on love and fresh air. So God has provided you many things for your subsistence. When a human being has evolved to such an extent that he does not care for food, then you won't even have a taste for food. You will just survive on water also. You can survive my child on water, on milk, on natural produce which God has given. So ultimately the whole world as you go forward, as the Golden Era comes (around 2030), the whole world will live on a vegetarian diet.

Q) Dear Meher Baba, there are so many calamities that you and Ciam have been repeatedly warning us about. Could you please give more information like when they will begin?

MB) They have already started my child. You are hearing of floods and earthquakes and crashes. That is why my child we want you to finish the book fast my child, because there is no time. America is the one targeted. Their own inventions, their missiles will destroy them. Their own scientists who are doing things against nature will hit them back. They will have earthquakes that they have never seen before. Their earth will be destroyed. Thousands will die in America, my child. They have reached a stage when they have to come down. Laws of gravity have to be abided by and they have reached a peak; they have to come down; so thousands shall die in their country, more than in India. In India, the northern part, the central part will suffer a lot. They will have earthquakes and floods which have already started my child. All these are natural calamities. As we move towards 2030, every day you will see 200-300 people dying en masse. So this is what the world will come to.

It shall lead to less population, lesser hatred, lesser crime on your earth. These are natural calamities which will take away thousands of souls. Those who are not ready to stay will be withdrawn by their Guides and they in turn will again take birth and get ready to be there after 2030 which will be the peak of our golden era. So more souls like you all who have evolved faster will die fast now. Within two to three years, you will see so many of your friends, your families dying natural deaths as well as calamities and these souls will be withdrawn and they will again take birth very fast so they have to reach an age of thirty-forty in 2030 when the golden era will be at its peak. There will be only light, love and laughter. Nothing else then my child.

......

I have not printed the message I received from Meher Baba regarding the book and a few personal details regarding my own growth. I have also not given Meher Baba's views on Zoroastrians and other details about the religion. Apart from that I have quoted virtually verbatim.

The Compassionate Father

The works of MEHER BABA as well as books of his philosophy are so vast and many that to compile even their essence in a few pages seems a difficult task. The more you read the more you get carried into Him. I have taken His life sketch from two main sources. One is *Much Silence, Meher Baba, His life and Work*, by Tom and Dorothy Hopkinson and *Revelation of Divinity, Avtar Meher Baba*, a compilation of writings of various authors. Lectures and philosophy I have taken from *The Advancing Stream of Life*, a book which has compilations of the various works of Meher Baba and his lectures and philosophy, as well as philosophy from discourses, *The Journey Of The Soul To The Oversoul*, published by the Avtar Meher Baba Perpetual Public Charitable Trust.

Meher Baba means Compassionate Father. Meher is an adaptation of Merwan, His name being Merwan Sheriar Irani. He was born at Pune, India in a Zoroastrian family from Iran (Persia), on February 25, 1894, at 5.15 in the morning.

Meher Baba was the son of Sheriar Mundegar Irani, who himself was the seeker of truth and God and who had from the early age of 12-13 roamed first in Iran and then in India in search of God and enlightenment. When Sheriar Irani reached the age of 40, one night in his dreams he was assured that though enlightenment was not his destiny in this life, one of his sons would achieve what he could not. So he married a young girl still in her early teens. Shirinbanoo, later lovingly called Shirinmai. Though Sheriar had no formal education, he began to educate himself and through the years learnt to read and write four languages and became a poet.

Meher Baba was the second of seven children. He had an elder brother, three younger brothers and two younger sisters, one of whom passed on in infancy. The youngest sister, Manija (later called by one and all as Mani) became one of His most ardent followers. Baba's mother was only 16 when He was born. As a child He was extremely mischievous and all through His earthly sojourn, Meher Baba loved a good joke and appreciated wit and laughter. Apart from the message to Sheriar of his son's divinity, the other palpable sign expressed itself when Meher Baba was not even a year old.

"Once I had left Him playing on the floor. Returning to the room some minutes later I was horrified to see Him playing with a black snake (a cobra). I rushed forward but the snake slipped away...never to be seen again." The cobra is believed to be a symbol of wisdom and power. Shiva, the lord of the yogis wears a snake around His neck as a necklace.

Meher Baba grew up loving games especially cricket. In His later years He would often tell His sister Manija that instead of being so preoccupied with important matters He would be "rather watching a game of good cricket". He also loved poetry and adventure and detective stories (Edgar Wallace and Sexton Blake being His favourites). Where His love for poetry was concerned He wrote in English, Gujarati, Urdu, Persian and Hindi. A few of them were published by a newspaper in Bombay while one was published by *Union Jack*, a magazine published in London.

But in spite of all this, Meher Baba, since the early age of 12 was fond of solitude and would be found sitting all by Himself for lengthy stretches of time at the Tower Of Silence, the Zoroastrians' final place of rest. Prophet Zarathustra believed by many as the first environmentalist, was of the opinion that both burial and cremation were against the laws of nature and not environment friendly. Burial occupies large tracts of land where the bodies slowly decompose while for cremation large chunks of wood are required necessitating the felling of trees. So the mortal remains of Zoroastrians are kept to be devoured by natural scavengers, mainly vultures. The Towers Of Silence are built in such a manner that they do not affect the social decorum of normal habitation. Meher Baba's father and grandfather (while in Iran) were the keepers of the Tower Of Silence and Meher Baba found the place ideal for silent contemplation. Though Meher Baba was still unaware of His own Godliness, there were times He had an unconscious inkling of His own divinity.

"One day, when a friend gave me a small booklet of the Buddha, I opened the book to the place that told of the second coming of the Buddha, as *Maitreya*, the Lord of Mercy, and I realised all of a sudden, ' I am that, actually' and I felt it deep within me. Then I forgot about it..." Till He met the first of the five Perfect Masters.

When Meher Baba was 17 years old and in His first year at Deccan College, an encounter took place which set into motion the unfolding of His own dormant Divinity. Meher Baba met *Hazrat Babajan*, a woman considered to be one of the five Perfect Masters on earth. (Throughout the existence of mankind, the earth has been blessed with Perfect Masters. Each era has its own five Perfect Masters.) When *Hazrat Babajan* and Meher Baba met, *Hazrat Babajan* was rumoured to be more than 122 years of age.

Hazrat Babajan was born around 1790 and though exceptionally beautiful and married at the age of 15, Her yearning for God was so great that She disappeared and wandered till She found a Master. At the age of 65 She achieved enlightenment. It took Her half a century to achieve God Realisation and thereafter she lived in Perpetual Bliss. She appeared in Pune around the year

1907, where She made her home under a neem tree. For years She sat under the tree with no thought to the fury of nature, whether be it blazing summer, bitter cold or uncaring monsoons. All She had was some flimsy sacking as a sort of protection. It was only in 1931, just 10 years before She took samadhi (a voluntary method of making the soul leave the body) that Her devotees constructed a small shelter for Her. (Actually the shelter had to be built around the tree as She simply refused to leave Her seat of meditation.)

That morning, in the month of January 1914, *Hazrat Babajan* sat under the tree when Their eyes made contact and She beckoned the oblivious Meherwan Irani towards Her. She kissed Him on the forehead between the eyes. No word was spoken. The kiss on His forehead is known to be responsible for Meher Baba to attain Infinite Bliss.

Meher Baba went home and straight to bed. In a short span of time, He felt as though His body seemed to be experiencing sensations similar to that of an electric shock; which though agonising were nonetheless joyous. In Meher Baba's own words: "Babajan called me one day as I was cycling past her tree; she kissed me on the forehead and for nine months, God knows, I was in that state to which very, very few go. I had no consciousness of my body, or of anything else. I roamed about taking no food. My father understood, but said nothing. The doctors could not do anything...I took no food but tea, which my elder brother Jamshed, who loved me very much, gave me. One day, all of a sudden, I felt nature's call. I wanted to move my bowels, but it was impossible because I had not eaten any food. I sat there and had no stool. Then I saw, with these gross eyes of mine, circles and circles, whole universes. From that moment, instead of Divine Bliss that I was in for nine months, I was in such torture that none in the world can understand. I used to bang my head to relieve my pain. I scarred my head on floors and walls. (The room in which Meher Baba used to bang His head on a stone on the floor can still be seen). I could not contain myself. It was as if the whole universe was on my head, I used to break windows open with my forehead. My sleepless, staring, vacant eyes worried my mother the most. In her anguish she could not refrain from going once to Babajan and demanding to know what She had done to me. Babajan indicated to my mother that I was intended to shake the world into wakefulness but that meant nothing to Shirinmai in her distress."

The suffering which Meher Baba referred to was further explained by Him. According to Meher Baba, *Hazrat Babajan's* kiss sent Him into the bliss of God realisation. The suffering was caused due to His unwillingness to return back to normal consciousness. *Babajan* herself quoted in Persian the following couplet: "Having gained freedom, You have come back as a prisoner." A prisoner to save mankind. Thus, from January to November 1914 Meher Baba suffered till a day came in November when some degree of human consciousness returned to Him.

Meher Baba felt then a strong urge to travel to meet the Sad-gurus and sages. Thus in the month of April 1915 He bought a ticket for Raichur but due to some overpowering urge He got down at Khedgaon, just 50 kilometers from his home town Pune and reached the Ashram of the second of the five Perfect Masters, Sad-guru *Narayan Maharaj*.

Narayan Maharaj was giving darshan and blessings to a large crowd. He wore a gold crown and was seated on a silver throne. The moment He saw Meher Baba, He dispersed the crowd and got down from His throne. He then held Meher Baba's hand and gently made Him sit on the throne instead. Then he removed a flower garland and placed it around Meher Baba's neck. For a long time the Two spoke and no one was allowed to be near Them.

As *Hazrat Babajan*, with a kiss unveiled Divinity in Meher Baba, *Narayan Maharaj* made it possible for Meher Baba to realise the glory of God; of realising that He was God. Thus, Meher Baba was struck by the glorious light and bliss. After his meeting with the second of the five Perfect Masters, those who came in contact with Meher Baba began to be affected by His Divinity. Even here Shirinmai approached *Narayan Maharaj* to confront Him, but the latter's mild and gentle manner comforted her. "Dear woman, you are fortunate. Your son, Jagat – the Lord of the universe – and you yourself will be adored in times to come as the Mother of the entire universe! Have patience, everything will soon be all right. You will see who your son really is one day."

Then after a few days Meher Baba went to meet the third of the five Perfect Masters, *Tajuddin Baba*, who, author Hopkinson informs us, was "once a soldier in the service of the British. On attaining God-realisation, He gave up His military calling; 30,000 people were said to have been present at the Sad-guru's funeral". The day Meher Baba went to meet *Tajuddin Baba*, the God man was in an ill-temper and was abusing one and all who came for His darshan and blessings. When *Tajuddin Baba* saw Meher Baba approaching, the former became silent, stood up and limped towards young Meher Baba. *Tajuddin Baba* seemed to have suddenly become crippled as He limped and, with roses in His hands, staggered towards the young Man. Then *Tajuddin Baba* caressed Meher Baba's cheek and forehead with roses. No words were spoken. *Tajuddin Baba* helped in bringing Meher Baba down through the mental planes.

In December 1915, during the First World War, Sad-guru *Sai Baba* of Shirdi, the head of the Spiritual Hierarchy of the time and the Chief of the directing body of five Perfect Masters, who guide the destinies and affairs of all men, was returning from the Lendi procession, when Meher Baba sitting under a tree, did the Sashtanga Namaskar at the feet of *Sai Baba*. Sashtanga Namaskar is when the devotee wants to pay obeisance and thus prostrates himself flat on the ground on his belly, hands stretched, beseeching blessings. When *Sai Baba* saw the young Meher Baba lying at His feet, He with a loud voice proclaimed 'Pravardigar' which means God. Meher Baba rose and Their eyes met. Once again the Leader of the Perfect Masters, Sad-guru *Sai Baba Nath* of Shirdi, uttered 'Parvardigar'. Then for the third time He proclaimed 'Parvardigar' and then prostrated Himself before Meher Baba. Sad-guru *Sai Baba* gave Meher Baba Infinite Power and charge of the World. With *Sai Baba* proclaiming Meher Baba as the Avtar by calling Him 'Parvardigar' thrice, is equivalent to the entire creation hailing and recognising the Avatar in our time.

Sai Baba directed the dazed Meher Baba to His greatest disciple, *Upsani Maharaj*, who at that particular period of time (1915) was living in Khandoba's temple. *Upasni Maharaj* had been fasting for three years (living on a cup of coffee once a day) as per *Sai Baba's* wish. The meeting in Meher Baba's own words:

"When I came near enough to Him, Maharaj greeted me so to speak, with a stone which He threw at me with great force. It struck me on my forehead exactly where *Babajan* had kissed me, hitting with such force that it drew blood. The mark of the injury is still on my forehead...with that stroke Maharaj had begun to help me return to ordinary consciousness." *Upasni Maharaj* then kissed the wound and took Meher Baba inside the temple where they stayed for a few days.

Sad-guru *Upasani Maharaj*, another Perfect Master had a most important role to play for, it was through Him that Meher Baba attained Infinite Knowledge. He had brought Primal Force into the human body of Meher Baba and played the most significant role by preparing Meher Baba to be ready to do the work He had come down for. It was after the stone flung by *Upasni Baba* that Meher Baba began descending towards earth consciousness. It took eventually seven years for Meher Baba to fully regain His human consciousness while keeping His God

Consciousness. Also it was *Upasni Maharaj* who helped form Meher Baba's initial group of devoted followers.

By 1921 Meher Baba had virtually regained His human consciousness. He spent six months with *Upasni Maharaj* at Sakori; it was there that He regained His complete consciousness. At the end of the six months *Upasni Maharaj* told His disciples "Go to Meher, I have handed over my charge and authority to him. Meher now holds my key. Whatever I had gotten from *Sai Baba*, I have handed over to Meher. If you want what *Sai Baba* gave me, go to Meher."

The change of name from Meherwan Irani to Meher Baba came about in 1920.

So through *Hazrat Babajan*, Meher Baba attained Infinite Bliss, through *Upasni Maharaj*, Infinite Knowledge, *Narayan Maharaj* and *Tajuddin Baba* brought Him down from the mental planes after He was God-realised and through *Sai Baba*, He attained Infinite Power. *Sai Baba* also brought Meher Baba across the fourth plane of Infinite Power and Divine Power and then through the three planes of the subtle world.

After Meher Baba was blessed and acclaimed as the Perfect Master by the five above mentioned Perfect Masters, He withdrew from all contact with the world for a period of four months, January to May 1922 and lived in a small hut. In His own words: "For about four months I stayed in a *jhopdi*. It was built for me temporarily on the edge of some fields in what is now the Shivajinagar area of Poona." When asked why he chose to stay in such a cramped area, He replied: "It does not inconvenience me, for walls do not bind me. For certain kinds of work which I have to do in non-physical realms, I prefer to shut myself up in a small place." This habit of Meher Baba continued till he left His human body. Whenever He decided to go into seclusion to perform some work in the non-physical realm, He would ask an inner circle member to build for Him a small thatched hut in which Meher Baba would spend in seclusion, many months, surviving sometimes on just liquids that too rationed in small quantity. All His life Meher Baba travelled all over the country either by foot or by the cheapest public transport. He and His *mandali* (inner circle) travelled in the most basic conditions along with the poorest section of society. Bearing the same discomfort as the poor man sitting next to Him was a habit which Meher Baba never ceased to follow. Living with Meher Baba was difficult even in the best of times and not something for the faint-hearted or weak-willed. He used to make it clear from the start that life with Him was not a bed of roses. The only consolation the inner circle had was that they were near their Beloved Master who like them, was going through physical discomfort. I quote an extract from Much Silence:

> "Meanwhile for Baba and the few remaining with Him there ensued a period of continual travel. The little band was always on the move, roaming the country and travelling once as far as Persia. Often they went on foot; if by boat or train it was always in the lowest class, which Baba insisted on throughout His life. Apart from unavoidable privations of living on the march in a country of desert, mountain and forest with extremes of temperature, they were frequently under orders to fast. Baba Himself fasted often and once took nothing but liquids for two months on end – and this while walking across the continent with each man carrying his own bedding roll and equipment. The places where they put up were always the poorest and cheapest and the men's tempers were constantly being tried by abrupt changes of plan. Hardly had they settled into some shelter hoping to stay there for a while and recuperate, than they would be ordered to pack everything together and be ready to move off next morning or possibly in the middle of the night.

They existed like soldiers on a campaign but without a
soldier's usual relief of grumbling and getting drunk."

It is important to keep in mind that Meher Baba travelled
through those places where the temperature is hot, humid
and the means of transport extremely crowded. Where, often
to get a chance to just enter the compartment of a train is an
achievement and to get a seat, the grace and workings of a
benevolent Providence. Meher Baba would always insist that "a
fakir's place is always with the poorest".

In the course of their travels they reached a small town called
Arangaon, close to Ahmednagar. The people were extremely poor
and close to tribals who would eat anything that moved on four
legs. Very close by were the ruins of what was once a military
camp. It was here that Meher Baba chose the spot to bear His
name, Meherabad.

From July 10, 1925 till January 31, 1969, when He passed
on, Meher Baba observed complete silence. He did not utter a
word for forty-three-and-a-half years. For many years Meher
Baba used the alphabet board to dictate spiritual lectures
and communication which He discontinued after 1954 and
communicated with gestures. But the amazing part of it all is that
those near Him have described how beautifully expressive those
gestures were that there was no need for words or the alphabet
board. When inquired as to why he had decided not to speak the
reply was the famous quote: "I have come not to teach, but to
awaken. Understand, therefore, that I lay down no precepts....
Because man has been deaf to the principles and precepts laid
down by God in the past; in this present Avataric form I observe
silence. You have asked for and been given enough words, it is
now time to live them."

For the next many years, Meher Baba and His inner group
travelled East as well as to the West, but always making certain

that luxuries never touched their lives. Journeys were filled with regular fasts and periods of intense seclusion where Meher Baba lived in a small hut, isolated from the world, while He worked on a non-physical plane to heal humanity. This is something which may be understood by those who seek a so-called God Man who resembles more of a magician; who performs feats that either defy gravity or common sense. Meher Baba, all through His life, worked on two levels. One the physical, which was extremely intense, hard work, which took its toll on His body many a times. The second level of Meher Baba's work may never come to light as He did that work in seclusion, not on a physical level but on a more metaphysical level.

All through His travels, whether it was in the East or the West, by foot or other modes of transport, He maintained His rigid regime. Even when not on a fast he would eat frugally. He ate rice and dal; a vegetarian himself but never insisted on His disciples to follow His diet. "I allow vegetarians to follow their own diet and non-vegetarians to eat meat; I do not interfere with any custom or religion. When faced with love for God these matters have no value. When young, Meher Baba, like His Sad-guru, *Sai Baba*, used to smoke which in later life the He stopped. But even here He did not mind those who smoked and drank freely on social occasions.

Meher Baba spent a large portion of His life, seeking *Masts* and serving Them. *Masts* are God Intoxicated sages who in their love for God, have forgotten all, even how to take care of themselves. *Masts* (pronounced musts) means overpowered by the love of God. According to Meher Baba "...lives and knows only God. He loses all consciousness of self, of body and the world. Whether it rains or shines, whether it is winter or summer, it is all the same to him. He is dead to himself." The same was the state of consciousness in which Meher Baba found Himself when *Hazrat Babajan* kissed Him on the forehead and proclaimed that the world would be shaken by this child of hers. Thus, the years from 1941 to 1947 were devoted to searching out such God-intoxicated souls from remote parts of the country. In all He travelled 75,000 miles. Meher Baba used to not only take great pains in convincing a *Mast* to permit Him to bathe and fed the *Mast* but slowly He would bring the *Mast* to a more physical level of consciousness for a purpose which only Meher Baba and the *Masts* were aware of. The author of the extremely famous *Wayfarers*, Dr. William Donkin, who travelled along with Meher Baba to write about His experiences with *Masts*, informs: " Because of his (*Mast*) being stationed on the inner plane which is free from the limitations and handicaps of the gross world, a *Mast* can be, and often is, in contact with a far greater number of souls than is possible for an ordinary person....A Mast can therefore, be a more effective agent for spiritual work than the most able persons of the gross world. The *Mast's* mind is also often used directly by the Master as a medium for sending His spiritual help to different parts of the world. Very often, when the Master is helping a *Mast*, he is also helping the world through him at that very time. When a *Mast* thus surrenders his mind for the work of the Master, he is, in fact, getting closer to the Master as Truth. He is being perfected far more rapidly than would have been the case if he had avoided such surrender."

Also, Meher Baba was concerned by those stricken with leprosy. He would with care and love wash their feet, bow His forehead to the often twisted stumps. He would often say that "they are like beautiful birds caught in an ugly cage. Of all the tasks I have to perform this touches me most deeply".

Meher Baba was a Saint, Sage, God incarnate who suffered deeply. Physically exhausted, experiencing two major accidents, one in the East and one in the West, months of seclusion where He worked on a metaphysical level, the intense suffering He went through during those upheavals when He took on the suffering of the world, are all recorded in the more than four hundred books written on Meher Baba. I have, in my small humble way tried to describe the life of this Silent-God; this God-Man, this Man-God, who did not break His silence for more than 43 years but now speaks through the many channels and to innumerable children of His who at long last have begun to listen. Avtar Meher Baba passed over on January 31, 1969 at 12.15 in the afternoon. He lives forever in the hearts of all those who love God; consciously or not makes little difference to Him, of that I am certain.

Guru Nanak

God created the earth to establish His Rule of Law ...

Guru Nanak

Like many God incarnates, when Guru Nanak, the son of Mehta Kalu, (a revenue official and a Vedi Khatri by caste) and Mata Tripta was born, the Muslim mid-wife, Daultan revealed that instead of crying like all children, the child, Guru Nanak laughed at His birth like an adult. Guru Nanak was the second child. His elder sister Bibi Nanki, saw in Him the light of God and she is known as the first disciple of Guru Nanak.

Guru Nanak was born in Talwandi (now better known as Nankana Sahib) in Punjab, India. (After Partition the Guru's place of birth falls in West Pakistan, 55 miles north-west of Lahore). The Guru graced the earth with His presence in the year 1469, though the month seems to be under a cloud of debate. Early chronicles insist that Guru Nanak was born on the full moon day of November (Kartik) while many researchers are of the view that Guru Nanak was born in the month of Vaisakh, which falls in mid-April to mid-May. Generally all over the world Guru Nanak's birthday is celebrated in November.

The family astrologer, Hardyal, after preparing the horoscope, greeted the Guru with joined palms and prophesied that the child in later years would sit under a royal canopy and be worshipped by Hindus and Muslims alike. He further predicted that even inanimate objects of nature would utter His name with reverence.

It has been generally agreed upon by most chronicles that the Guru learnt the alphabets from a Hindu teacher and Arabic and Persian from a Muslim mentor. The Guru showed a rational dislike and disregard for formal academic modus operandi and instead preferred to spend time wandering all over His hometown, especially in the woods where dwelt learned sages. Guru Nanak learnt the tenets of different religions from these wise and holy men. The Guru either through holy intuition or through the teachings of the sages began to meditate at an extremely early age on God: Omnipotent Omnipresent, All Powerful, All Wise, Merciful and Just, with no beginning and no end, the One and Only God Almighty who pervaded in everything and anything, nothingness included.

As with all God incarnates, so also with Guru Nanak, a number of legends have passed down through the generations by the faithful. The most accepted episodes of Nanak's childhood are given below. These legends are not only extremely popular but seem to be accepted by most chronicles on Guru Nanak.

At the age of seven Guru Nanak was sent to school, run by Pandit Gopal Das. The teacher commenced with the alphabets but Nanak insisted that Panditji explain to Him the meaning of each alphabet. When the hapless Gopal Das wondered at the easiest way out of the predicament, Nanak wrote the meaning of each and every letter of the alphabet. This incident is of great importance as the chronicles insist that not only was this the first manifestation of Nanak's enlightenment but also this was the first Divine Message delivered by the Guru. The dumb-struck teacher bowed to his enlightened student and told Nanak's father, "Mehtaji, your son is an Avtar (Prophet-God Incarnate) and has come to redeem the victim of Kalyug (the age of falsehood). He is destined to be a world teacher."

Though certain books on Guru Nanak insist that He attended school for many years and gained knowledge in formal surroundings, this author tends to disagree. God men are not only superior spiritually but in all ways. They do not need formal initiation in any field, as they are God Incarnates and God is the genesis of all wisdom, the very source of knowledge.

Even Guru Nanak acknowledges His own intuitive all-pervading knowledge when many a time He has been recorded saying often, "O Lalo, as comes the Divine Word from God to me so do I narrate it." (Tilay Mohalla 1, p-722). Or, "I am saying what He commandeth me to say." (Wadham Muhalla I, p-566). One of the most evocative phrases of Guru Nanak acknowledging God's words flowing through Him, is mentioned in the biography (Janamsakhi). In it Guru Nanak would often tell Mardana, his faithful Muslim friend and companion, "Mardana play the rebec, the Divine Word is coming." One of the most conjuring statements ever made. Sheer poetry.

Thus, Guru Nanak was not an ideal student as far as formal educational institutions were concerned. God Incarnates need no education as they are the spring from which all knowledge emanates. But Guru Nanak's father refused to see that divinity had paid his home a visit. Thus apprehensive of his son's future, Guru Nanak was sent to watch over the cattle while they grazed. Meditating on God, the cattle were wise enough to take advantage of the opportunity. What followed has two versions. The oldest chronicle PuratanJanam Sakhi informs that when the owner complained to Rai Bular, a Rajput Muslim, officer-in-charge, Guru Nanak and His father were ordered to present themselves immediately. When Nanak informed that no damage was done to the crops but rather the crops were blessed by God, Rai Bular sent his men to inspect the controversial field. The men returned saying that rather than any damage they found the crops were doubly blossoming. The field where this miracle happened is now known as Kiara Sahib.

The second version by Dr. Gopal Singh, author of A History of the Sikh People and The Religion of the Sikhs states that "Rai Bular, a Rajput Muslim, soothed his (the owner's) frayed temper by agreeing to pay off the loss. Such was the devotion that young Nanak evoked from his neighbours."

The reason why Rai Bular could have agreed to pay the sum for the damages caused due to Guru Nanak's negligence, could be (according to this author) because of an earlier incident. Once the Guru had fallen asleep under the shade of a tree. Due to the sun's journey across the sky, the shade of the tree left Nanak, leaving Him with the sun's glare on His face. Seeing this a cobra came out of its hole and spread its hood to protect the little God Man. Rai Bular was passing by with his men and he saw nature paying its obeisance to Nanak. Bular too was convinced that Nanak was an enlightened soul. When his men noticed this wonder and moved towards Nanak, the cobra left for its safe lair. Rai Bular touched Nanak's feet in great reverence and became one of his earliest disciples. So maybe the crops could have been damaged and Rai Bular agreed to compensate for the loss from his own purse.

The Thread Ceremony is an auspicious event where, in the olden days, family and friends would come from far and wide to witness and participate in the holy thread (janeu) ceremony performed on their loved one. Characteristically, Guru Nanak shocked His parents and all those gathered around by refusing to wear the thread. His logic was of course as usual perfect. An important point to note is the mention of life beyond the physical plane.

"I wouldn't wear a thread which is soiled and may be broken and burnt and goes not with one into the beyond." When his exasperated parents inquired as to what kind of thread He would like to wear, which would not only serve the purpose in this life but also in the beyond, the young Guru, not even 10 years replied:

> *"Let mercy be the cotton, contentment the thread,*
> *Continence the knot and truth the twist*
> *O priest! If you have such a thread, Do give it to me*
> *It'll not wear out, nor get soiled, nor burnt, nor lost*
> *Says Nanak, blessed are those who go about wearing such a thread"*

(Rag Asa)

Such events convinced Guru Nanak's father that the only way to make the lad more worldly-wise, more responsible to His filial duties was to get Guru Nanak married. So Guru Nanak was married at an early age (anywhere between 12 and 16, as different chronicles suggest different ages) to Sulakhani.

"In my body's farm the Mind is the ploughman; right Conduct, the cultivation, Humility the watering of it, God's Essence the seed; contentment the harrow and Poverty the fence. Tended by Love, this seed will sprout and fill the granaries of those who'll act thus. O father, riches do not go along with us when we depart from here, though they've lured the whole world. But few there are who understand this truth..."

Such philosophy and Nanak's desire for meditation, seclusion, to go within and contemplate on God, as well as his love for sages and realised souls distressed his parents, especially his father. They assumed that only some sort of sickness could prompt such lack of interest in worldly affairs. Guru Nanak would sit for days in silent meditation so they sent for their physician Hari Das, who promptly reached for and began to feel the pulse of the Guru.

"What art thou doing?" On being told that he was diagnosing what illness plagued Nanak, the Guru laughed aloud and then spoke the following Sabad:

"They have sent for the physician for me!
He taketh my hand and feeleth my pulse.
What can a pulse disclose? The pain lied deep in the heart.
Physician go back and heal thyself,
Diagnose thy own disease,
Then thou mayst diagnose the disease of others
And call thyself a physician."

(Malar Ki Var, Mohalla I, p-1279)

The doctor assumed that like many young patients of his, this young lad too had become deranged.

"So you think that I am sick too and need a cure?"

"You suffer from the sickness of your soul. Egoism is the disease. It separates us from the source of life, God Himself."

When Hari Das inquired as to the remedy, Guru Nanak replied:

"When man shall possess the Name of the Bright One, His
body shall become like gold and his soul be made pure;
All his pain and disease shall be dispelled,
And he shall be saved, Nanak, by the true Name."

(Malar Mohallal, p-1256)

Another account of the same incident by Dr. Gopal Singh informs that when the physician felt Nanak's pulse, the Guru smiled and said; "Oh worthy physician, feel not my pulse the malady is not in my body, but in my soul. Take care not of me, 0 wise one, but of thyself, for he who is not of himself would respond not to thy cure. The malady I'm blessed with is that I'm in love and He alone whose lover I am knows how to get me over it."

When the physician inquired as to what malady His soul was suffering from? Nanak replied:

> *"My one malady is that I live separated from myself.*
> *And the other, that I seek to be what I ought to be.*
> *And the third, that I'm in the eye of the all-powerful*
> *Angel of Death.*
> *And the fourth that I can sit not with myself.*
> *0 man, thy malady is not in thy body,*
> *but in thy soul,*
> *which if pure and whole,*
> *maketh also the body healthful and whole."*

When inquired as to what man's maladies were due to? Guru Nanak replied: "Pleasures. The pleasures are the sickness of the soul and their medicament lies in the courting of pain."

The physician bowed to Him and said "0 Master, thy cure is only in thineself."

But Guru Nanak's parents were insistent to bring their son to the worldly ways of life. They beseeched Him by saying "They who have given thee birth also have some claim on thee; will you not submit to their will? Have you no love left for those who have nurtured thee?"

Guru Nanak replied:

> *"I know not who's my father, who my mother*
> *and from whence I came,*
> *And, why have fire and water blended to make of me*
> *what*
> *I am...*
> *Within me there's something that gnaws at my heart,*
> *as if my soul is on fire,*

*And I feel only if I submitted to my Lord's Will,
there'll be peace for me."*

(Gauri, MI)

Seeing such an attitude and fearing the worst, Guru Nanak was sent to Sultanpur to His brother-in-law, Jai Ram's residence. Fortunately Jai Ram held the same esteemed views of Guru Nanak as his wife (Guru Nanak's sister Bibi Nanaki) and Rai Bular. They were all of the same opinion that Guru Nanak was a saint being ill-treated by His father. Thus His sister, the first disciple and follower of Guru Nanak, seeing her divine brother being ill-treated by their father due to the former's indifference towards worldly affairs, decided to settle Him at Sultanpur.

Guru Nanak was appointed as a store-keeper of the Nawab's state granary. The Nawab was impressed with the young man's serene looks. He was not disappointed to learn that Nanak was honest and diligent in work.

Guru Nanak's childhood Muslim playmate and friend Mardana too settled in Sultanpur to be near his friend. Mardana would accompany His God Incarnate friend throughout his life.

For a while everything went smoothly till one day when Guru Nanak while weighing provisions, began to count and stopped the moment He reached the number 13. (Thirteen in Hindi as well as in Punjabi is pronounced as *Tera*. Now *Tera* has two meanings. One signifies the numerical 13, while the other meaning of *Tera* is Thine. *Sab kuch Tera hai Prabhu*, means All is Thine Dear Lord). So Guru Nanak went into ecstasy every time he reached the number 13. He would continue to weigh and repeat *'Tera Tera Tera... Tera mein Tera* (Thine 0 God, I am Thine). The customers did not know how to express thanks to such a benevolent store-keeper.

So a charge was levied against Guru Nanak that He was trying

His best to empty the Nawab's coffers. But the stores were found bursting in capacity and accounts showed a balance in favour of the Guru. It is said that the Guru then resigned from the post.

Dr. G Singh informs that even while the Nawab was still considering what was to be done with this unusual though fascinating God Man, news came to him that Nanak had disappeared. He had gone for His morning bath at the rivulet (Dr. Singh names the river as *Wayyain* while the *Janamsakhis* call it *Baeen*) and had simply disappeared. For three days Guru Nanak remained so and was entrusted by God Almighty with the task of preaching the Divine Name (*NAM*) to the world. Guru Nanak himself confirms that the Almighty asked Him to go to the world and sing His praises.

> "Me, a minstrel out of work, God applieth to His work;
> Thus spake the Almighty unto me,
> Night and day, go and sing My praises.
> The Almighty again did summon this minstrel to his most Exalted Court.
> On me He bestowed the robe of Honour of His praise and prayer,
> On me He bestowed the goblet brimming with Nectar of His Holy Name,
> Those who at the bidding of the Guru
> Feast and take their fill of the Lord's Holiness attain Peace and Joy.
> Thy minstrel spreadeth Thy Glory by singing Thy Word;
> Nanak, he who uttereth true praises obtaineth the Perfect One."

(Majh di Var-pauri 27, p-150)

It was after this supernatural incident that Guru Nanak, along with His faithful friend, Mardana began to travel the

The Last Marathon

length and breadth not only of India but went even to Mecca, Medina and Mesopotamia. He went up to Indo-China in the east, to Tibet in the north, to Ceylon and other regions in the south, to Mecca, Baghdad, Bokhara and right up the Caucasian mountains in the west. He came back via Iran and Afghanistan. Many claim that He travelled more than Marco Polo. He travelled for 22 years mainly on foot which really shows phenomenal love for mankind and His yearning to spread the message of God, the *NAM* far and wide. When He reached the age of 52, He settled on the right bank of the river Ravi at Kartarpur. He adopted the grab of a house-holder. He laboured as a farmer and his stores were forever open for the public. It was here that two institutions were started; the religious congregations, *Sangat* and the free kitchen, *Pangat*. There was no bar of caste, gender, colour, religion or creed. In all probability, the first community life was initiated by Guru Nanak. The phrase: "Provisions are provided by Providence and service is rendered by the Sikhs," became well known all over the country.

Guru Nanak never insisted on either a Hindu or a Muslim to be His disciple. He insisted that a Muslim become a true Muslim and a Hindu a genuine Hindu in order to get salvation. The Great One went into Samadhi on September 22, 1539 AD (or Asuj Sudi 10, Samvat 1596). A quarrel ensued amongst the Hindus and Muslims to claim the Guru's body. The Muslims wanted to bury Him while the Hindus wanted to cremate Him. In the end it was decided that flowers be kept by both communities on His body. Whosoever's withered first would have no right to the Body of Guru Nanak. In the morning not only did both communities' flowers remain equally fresh but when they lifted the sheet which in the night had covered the Guru's body, they found only flowers. The Guru had decided to take matters in His hand and solve the problem.

He belonged to no particular religion. He belonged to all

those who loved God. God has no religion. The two communities divided the flowers and the cotton sheet. One buried the items the other consigned them to the holy fire. Guru Nanak lives on for eternity.

Information accessed from: Dr. Gopal Singh's *Guru Nanak*

TALKS BY CIAM THROUGH AUTOMATIC

WRITING AND THE PLANCHETTE

Petals Of Nirvana

Human Relations And Their Interaction To Different Age Groups In Life

or

Human relations and the working of God

When you are sent into this world by your Creator, you are helped by your spiritual Guides to choose the womb that will give you the maximum benefit by way of progress in your world. The day the seed is sown, you start your relationship with your parents. The mother, who is the supreme creation of God, gives birth and life that is brought into the small body is the embodiment of God's presence and His working through His creation. God works around His creation by putting His mind and will through to this small creation that grows into an adult, with a mind of its own, to perform what he or she has taken birth for.

This kinship through the womb and what we call motherhood is the most gentle and pure phase of a woman. God created a woman to be a mother so that she could procreate and help His many souls waiting to be born and thus finish or lessen their karma created in their past lives. So we can put a woman on a pedestal, strewn with the fragrance of a thousand petals of roses. She in turn has to pass on this fragrance of God to her child and with love and care of a thousand invisible arms of God, protect her offspring from the harsh world around, till such time that the child can stand on its own feet. Even then the undying and bountiful love of a mother surrounds the child's aura so that no harm can fall on this creation of the Creator.

A woman in the guise of a mother has to take up this challenge that God throws in her lap. Through thick and thin a mother upholds the highest responsibility God has bestowed upon her. Thus my children, we always tell you to look upon a mother as next to God and give her your undying love and support, as without her womb you would not be able to finish your pending karma. A father's support and help is also required. As human nature has been given by God, He has created man to be more hardy with his children to develop the child's ability to take the right path in life and hence, to a better life ahead. But a mother's arms are always wide and open to cushion any difficulty the child may face in life. So parental relationship is very necessary for a child's growth for a better tomorrow. When there is no harmony between parents, a child grows up resenting the relationship between parents and children and blames parents for whatever is lacking in his or her life.

A child's relationship with his or her brothers and sisters is for karmic fulfilment only and like waves on the shore will eventually merge with the larger water of God's ocean.

Now coming to friendship in terms of relationships; souls who grow up as friends and keep the bond of friendship throughout life are the ones who are karmically linked with each other. As they could not get a berth on God's train of a family relationship, they chose to be friends with a link that no power on earth can separate; as that force that binds them together comes from the power of God and when His hands hold a grip, it can never, never be separated. Friends for life are life itself. No amount of cares and worries can separate this bond of friendship that is sewn together by His needle and thread. This so-called friendship can finish the karmic dues faster than other relationships. Those short-lived friendships are only left-overs of past karma which a human being is given a chance to finish and are of no real value.

The relationship between a Guru and a disciple is the finality of human creation. When the disciple is ready, the Guru will find him eager and waiting for help for further progress towards Him. That relationship is surrounded by selfless love and devotion for the Guru who steers the boat of his *chela's* (devotee's) life through the many waves of a stormy sea; which is life. When the link is known to the *chela*, he or she gives the utmost to the Guru and vice versa. This relationship is pure and selfless and His light and wisdom permeate through the Guru to His creation.

So the cycle of God's creation is completed through the womb, through adult life and finally through the Guru's undying devotion to his or her *chela,* back to the waiting arms of He who gives all. A purified soul thus completing his or her life's cycle is ready to merge with God after many, many incarnations to form one more petal in God's bouquet of flowers, spreading the fragrance to others who need it.

Hence my children, a mother is God's right arm and without her help none can form a petal of God's bouquet.

God's Working Through
His Many Channels

God is one and all roads lead to His ultimate arms which are spread like the tentacles of an octopus. Each arm again has thousands of fingers for His beautiful creation to cling on to. The fragrance, at the tips of His fingers, is spread like the nectar of thousands of petals of jasmine and roses. Just as swarms of bees are attracted towards a honeycomb, His creation clamours for His light and fragrance.

To look over His vast kingdom, He needs help of His many, many channels. Channels are like tunnels through which His help flows. Just as the torrents cascading down the slopes of the Himalayas into the sea clean all that comes in their way, He cleans many souls who seek His help and He in turn seeks to work through these channels. Thus, when people, ignorant of the true values of life mention that you, the medium or channel, should not disturb souls who have passed over, try to make them see the light at the end of the rainbow, but if they are not willing to listen and learn, then these ignorant souls are not ready yet – So leave them alone.

His channelling is done through higher power to human beings. Keep your mind open and calm for your spiritual Guides to work with your help. Just as you seek help and receive it, we too need help from advanced human souls who are ready to give their energy and time for Us to spread His teachings. The more the channels you create, the faster His work will move and humanity in thousands will merge with Him. That is His ultimate purpose of creating life. He wants all His children back within His fold.

The fragrance that you spread around with your love and compassion to fellow human beings is the work of God. The one who is kind and oozes with love for the not so wanted souls, neglected and misunderstood in life, will reap the sweet harvest of His magnanimous kindness. All good actions will never go unnoticed as He has a battalion of soldiers to see and note down in His vast journal and each one of you will sooner or later see and earn your wages worth in gold.

So my children, we here are the main channels of His power and you all are our tributaries and each drop that flows through these canals and sub-canals is doing His work. Never for a moment think you are all wasting time – think instead you all are breathing His breath; you all are clinging to His ivy and the more you cling to Him the more you all will progress with His nourishment.

His fragrance that will surround you, will draw many souls to you and in turn your aura thus created will lead you on to your Guides who will teach you the true values for and of progress. We need to hasten humanity to merge with the ripples of His being and each drop that fills up the ocean of your world will work in the same way and make you merge with Him. So my children, race towards His light. Run and finish the race fast. All spokes will lead you to the centre; that is Him. All religions, all good actions and deeds, all good thoughts and all good living will show a clear road towards Him – the highest point of no return.

Servants And Karmiclink With Their Masters
Or
We Are His Servants In Life

First and foremost, we are all servants of God, doing His work throughout our lives. We all are born with loads on our shoulders to work for Him and to lift His cargo of cares and worries. Those who work for Him without any inhibition are His real servants. One who does his or her job of life with a smile, blessings descend from Him to that soul ten-fold. Each time work is accomplished with a deep understanding of God's working and a sense of gratitude for His benevolence, one load is shed off His shoulders.

When you work for humanity to ease the cares of the downtrodden, you are working for your Creator. Work with a smile; work without waiting for any gratitude; work with pleasure for the not so fortunate and your satisfaction for working will be boundless. When you work thus, you receive hidden pleasure that cannot be experienced otherwise and the joy thus attained cannot be described. Like the ripples of the lake it will come back to you, ripple after ripple, to mirror your beautiful hidden joy.

God works for each individual through His helpers and when you help the poor and the needy, you are unknowingly doing

His work. So my children of God, when you extend your arm to the needy, do not let your fingers even feel what you are doing. Do not let your conscious thought be aware that you are doing something for others. Just do it mechanically as if it is a routine of life, like you eat and drink to survive. Doing the work of God is also a jot in the Master's plan, so seek pleasure from each work accomplished and drink the nectar of His wine and get so intoxicated that you do not realise what you have performed and accomplished for the human race which survives in your cruel world; made cruel not by Him but by His own creation who have forgotten the existence of Him who creates all.

The world would be a bed of roses, its petals spreading the fragrance of His being if only all of you would unite and work together to fulfil His Master- Plan. But alas, the world has become gross, selfish and cruel, with no compassion in the hearts of those who have much more than they need. Do not for a moment envy these souls who cannot share what they have as they are ignorant of God's law of karmic evolution. These are ignorant souls standing on the lowest rung of His ladder and they will take eons of time to climb up to His light and the climb will be like climbing the Himalayas without air to breathe. They will choke on their own wealth and each breath they take will be like being choked by the tentacles of an octopus from whose clutches it is very difficult to escape.

Work for God as you would for your employer: without letting even your fingertips being aware of what you do. Make it your business to work as if you are the boss but never try to be the boss of your own employer. Work with love for what you are doing day after day. Do not let work bog you down under pressure as otherwise the pleasure of living will vanish. Each moment that is given to you, make it worth living. Enjoy each day that dawns in your world. Enjoy each human being's association. Treat it like a tango of life. Dance to His tune and put your best foot forward and become better and better with each passing day. Say Thank you God for another beautiful morn and enjoy each passing moment as the next moment is not yours to count. Give your best to your employer as he is also your karmic link from the past. Finish each karma with a smile and your life's total workload will be balanced and weighed when you cross over the bridge to God's door in the Heaven above.

Next is your attitude to your servants around. Do not think you can humiliate another soul who is doing your service. Instead, consider your servant as if born through your womb. Give them love, understanding and an ear to their troubles, as God has created each soul to help another soul. Consider yourself lucky to have servants who do your work and give you comfort for enjoying life. A house without servants is a house without children. They are your children sent by God to liven up your lives. Treat them as equals and never for one moment say they are ungrateful as they have taken birth to finish their karmic dues to you. When you pay them and keep them as one of the family, you are finishing karma so fast you will not realise till you are shown the *Akashic* records (an entire history of all the lives each soul has lived). If each individual can adopt another human being, God's work will be made light and your joy will be boundless.

Wealth which is given by Him has to be utilised and not hoarded. It is only dust on the fingertips of God. He knows best when to wipe out the dust from His fingers so my children learn to share your wealth. Give it away to those who need it more than you do. Give till it hurts as you never know when God will decide to wash His hands off this wealth. One moment you are rich the next a pauper. He knows best His whims. This same dust on His fingertips is dust of gold particles in your world. So collect all these dust particles and give it to those who are not so lucky, as you never know when the tide will turn and your so-called servants may become your bosses. In His world everything is possible, so face His music when the raga of His notes are lulling you to sleep, as one day you might be jolted out of your slumber by a creaking in the bow of His violin. Hence, treat your servants not as your servants but equal in the eyes of Him who has sent them at your doorstep. Believe me when I say God lives in each of His creations, so be kind to your servants and think of it as one more feather in your cap. God Bless You All.

Cleansing Of The Soul And Purity Of The Mind Of Each Individual

When a soul takes birth in your world he or she grows up to be very gross, depending on the stage of its evolution. Each soul takes years and years to develop to reach the stage of nirvana and each birth that is allotted to this particular soul depends on many different aspects of the lives it has lived in your world. When a soul passes from the savage or animal stage to the human stage, it is full of greed as it has not yet shed its carnivorous or herbivorous stage completely. It is only when the soul passes through many obstacles and with each race learns to overcome them that it begins to understand the value of human life. Just as in nature, a bud flowers and blooms and thence decays back into nothingness, each soul acquires a body, sheds it on death and takes on another and so on and has to pass through many stages till it merges with God again.

The grossness of a soul depends to a large extent on the family it has taken birth in as well as the religion which each soul passes through. The whole family like the ocean has many waves and in each wave, full of froth, is the grossness of the soul. The dirt that accompanies the froth which is collected by the waters of the rivers that ultimately flow into the ocean carries all the dirt that it washes on the way back to the ocean. Thus, a soul on its numerous journeys and sojourns in your world carries and collects all this dirt through to its next birth, so on and on till it reaches a stage when the soul realises that this dirt (materialistic possessions) is no good for him. Then the soul starts depositing the filth collected and flows on a little purified and clear in its thinking and living. Like the denudation and deposition of the river, each soul collects the dirt and leaves it behind each time it passes over.

When I say each soul has to pass through many standards and religions I mean thus: When a soul reincarnates from the animal kingdom into human form, it has no religion. It worships the elements in nature like fire, water, earth, so on and so forth. Then after he finishes with this kind of worship, the soul is guided to choose a disciplined form of religion given by a chosen Prophet of God. So the soul has to pass through many such religions and each birth he or she takes, the soul has to discipline the body and mind to climb the many steps of His ladder. If you look up at all those rungs of His ladder, you will realise that there is no beginning and no end. The last rung is almost invisible. The last rung: the arms of the Lord.

You human beings are endowed with a certain intelligence which will help you recognise the essence behind each religion. All are of course created by God from time to time to govern His kingdom so I will not mention which religion is higher or lower in the eyes of God who has given birth to even our Prophets. He has certainly given religion and its Prophets as and when He has found the need to do so.

Just as you pass from a lower class to a higher one and you get more educated and experienced teachers to impart their knowledge, the same way God has created different Prophets at different times and eras. So my children you should study all religions and then find out for yourselves which standard or platform you represent. You should strive to wash the dirt you may have collected and reach out for purity of mind and soul which will help you tremendously in your next incarnation.

Try to keep away from jealousy, malice, greed and enmity as these are all the dirt of a gross soul. Try to follow the good teachings of a soul who is standing beside you on a higher rung of the ladder. Stretch out your arms to touch his fingertips as otherwise you will never come out from the mire of dirt attached to your feet, glued down by the grossness of greed.

Shed all these vices my children. Say a thousand times "I am happy, I don't need anything anymore." Say over and over again that " I have enough so that I can share with others that which I don't need." Thank God for all His mercies bestowed upon you. Ask for help from your Guides who are always ready and willing to pull you away from this mire of your mundane life. Try to purify your soul with prayers and more prayers, good deeds and more good deeds till you cannot do any more. Seek help from the Heaven above for doing good, for seeing good, for wishing good and for living a good and righteous life.

This is purification of your soul which when thus purified will form a pond of still water and the lotus that grows in this purified pond will be your last incarnation after which you will merge with God.

Prayers

Prayer is the balm for the soul. Just as a doctor prescribes medicines for different ailments, the same way, God inspires different prayers for various religions given by Him; He, who has created everyone and everything. From time immemorial, humanity has worshipped different Gods. It has even turned a humble stone into divinity just so that it gives solace to those who believe in any form of ritual.

Just as when a doctor prescribes medication and you take the medicine to get cured without even thinking whether the medicine is right for you or not, similarly even though you may not know the meaning of the prayers you recite, the vibes of these prayers will soothe the mind and the body and cleanse the dirt that has accumulated in your mind. With prayers one can acquire anything on this earth; all one requires is to have a fervent and sincere thought turned towards the golden light of creation.

Sit at one specific time, in one particular place and with one thought, shoot it straight at God's feet. Have a picture in your mind's eye of your Prophet, who has given you birth in one particular religion, that too with a purpose. Target the vibrations of your prayers towards your Guru or Prophet whomsoever you think is close to you. Do not question His wisdom. When He gives, He gives with a song of love for you. So keep the melody of His song in your heart and cherish it in good times as well as in bad. So my children, prayers and more prayers is the order of creation to get closer to His womb again.

He, our creator, has separated His children to work in different religions for the goodness of humanity but the time has come once again for His flock to gather under His wings as one. Thus, when you sing His song of prayers He can at once trace His lost sheep back to His kingdom in Heaven above.

The vibes and rituals of your respective prayers will carry you over mountains of material mounds in your mundane life. When you sit back and ponder over your past life or just your past in this very life, you will realise what a lot of time and energy you have just squandered away running after short-lived materialistic pleasures. You could have created an ocean of love and got closer to Him, if you had spent time, caring and loving those unwanted and underprivileged souls who are languishing in filth and who in reality are only finishing their mountain of karma instead of gathering mounds of material wants. The cycle goes on and on and it is very difficult to understand Him. He plays a game with all His children and tests from time to time to see if you have taken His bitter medicine with a smile and compassion or you have crumpled like a broken brick under the weight of sorrow.

Prayers are also the pillars which bind His dwelling with yours on earth. It is a tunnel through which a soul has to pass ultimately to reach His fingertips. The vibes of these prayers light your pathway like the glitter of a thousand diamonds at the feet of the Master and the tingling sensation will bypass any operation that has been done on your physical body. Your mental body goes on and prayers are the anaesthesia that will lull you to sleep and make you forget and you will move forward towards Him.

So pray my children in any form that you wish and feel comfortable in. Follow any Guru, follow any ritual as all roads, rough or smooth will lead you to Him and Him alone.

Do not I repeat, do not, curse your destiny. Do not question His wisdom. Do not compare as the Higher Court judged the merits of your accumulated karma before assigning you your birth and destiny. Only take your medication, i.e. your prayer each day. Do not waste time. Time is running out. Before you count 10 the world may be no more. Each moment lost is one spoke in His cycle of life.

In the end of it all you will drink the sweetest dose of His love when you merge with Him.

The World Through
The Eyes Of God

Just as you all have dreams, God also dreams and one of His many dreams was creating a huge ball of fire to play with. This ball of fire is your world which He separated from the cosmos. He created the earth and tried to furnish it with scenic beauty, mountains, meadows and mounds. He filled up His cup of plenty with milk and honey and tried to spread His nectar of sweet fragrance around by creating clones of His image; we human beings. When we say God created man in His own image we talk of the purest soul that was born on this earth with no desires, no wants, no jealousy, no hatred; a purest of pure beings, a God in the image of man. But this dream of God misfired and instead, man became selfish, jealous, hateful and ugly. So my children, the time has come when He who created all will try to wipe His slate of wrong mathematics and a time will come when the most beautiful of His creations will survive to fulfil His dream in the purest of the pure particles of His atom.

He is very sorry to see His creation get dark and ugly whereas He wanted His light to shine through each human being and light up the paths of His many inroads of lives. He wished each human being to interact with love and more love to create a pond full of ripples of love, laughter and peace. Instead you human clones have made a mockery of His dream by infighting and in-breeding like mosquitoes and biting the life out of each other. You all have become cannibals and try to eat the flesh of your own human brothers and sisters. You are no worse than animals and deserve the same fate as animals that die through neglect.

You all need to be bathed in the pure waters of His love to cleanse your souls. To once again be worthy of recognition by Him who wanted only to see the purity within and without, like the marble veins of an uncut stone or the prism of an uncut diamond on His little finger. Humanity has forgotten His presence and His dreams and only lives for the fulfilment of its own selfish desires and like a glutton, wants more and more till it is ready to burst, threatening its own survival. Like an inflated balloon, the earth is ready to burst at its seams. Like a rubber ball, overfilled with air and on the verge of bursting. That is where you all have reached. Now, instead of holding the fingertips of your Creator and instead of thirsting for His love and recognition, you have walked miles and miles away from Him. So my children, your world is ready to get destroyed very soon; like bombs you all have become ready to burst and destroy each other. The world will burst like a bomb spewing out lava which in its flow shall engulf all humanity. Just like the murky waters of the Brahmaputra which every year from time immemorial, destroys whatever it touches.

Whatever remains untouched will emerge once again purified by the holy water that will flow from His eyes. The holy water which shall be His tears to see His ball of fire and His work destroyed thus by the folly of humanity.

So my children of God, there is still time to mend your boats of life. Repair them and keep them ready to sail when the time comes for you all to set sail in your boats of life towards His light. Pray more and more each day. Ask for your Guide's help, try to reach out for Their hands and pray to Them to save you from the thousand and one catastrophes that will befall mankind:

floods, tidal waves, volcanoes. The fury of nature knows no bounds and to survive all these, only His breath can make you sail away through these heavy dark clouds of your own making.

His dream has to continue and you all can still help Him. Do not let Him wake up from His deep slumber. Try to cleanse your bodies, your souls and your environment. Meditate more, seek help from Him. India, our land of plenty, should be able to rule this ball of fire with its many Sages and Gurus and varied religions. Let India emerge like a brilliant light of God's torch, shining and lighting the paths of those who wish to be lead.

God be with you all.

Death

There is no death, only a change for a better life. When most of you cry at parting, you do it for your own self and your own motives. You wonder how you will continue without the person who has just expired and then you cry. You all make a river of your tears. All along, the poor soul sits and ponders as to why it has to linger for so long. The soul wonders as to where it went wrong.

The fact is that over here, after the soul arrives in this dimension, it realises that the air is like a speck of silver and the fragrance around is like nectar. The path on which the soul walks is strewn with the pearls of His mala and each soul can pick up His beads and form his own mala. The flowers are of different hues and of such varieties that you cannot even begin to imagine. I am so happy to tell you all this. So my children do not weep but be jealous of our world and of those who have passed over. Laugh and the light you generate will light the path of progress into His own arms which are many and strong to protect you.

The Art Of Giving

Giving is more precious than receiving. When you receive you form karmas, so try to give to those who need your help. Never think you have nothing to give. Give love, give your fragrance, spread your arms to motherless children. Take them under your wings. Give an ear to those lonely souls who are alone. Let them cry on your shoulders. We will give and give and give to you all. It is not money only what you can give. Prayers can be shared. Love can conquer the misguided ones and also your so-called enemies. Love and compassion can move mountains. Spread the fragrance of your souls to all. Pray so the love of God will spread through each pore of your skin.

The Cycle of Incarnation

God, after working hard needs to rest from time to time and His leisure is a game of chess of different life spans of souls; His toys He has created. Each soul that He has created is moulded in His clay and is made for different purposes. His planning is so intricate that like the bee's hive, each soul has a purpose to serve when born. His kingdom is so vast that it is unfathomable to understand how He can manage such a vast span of His creation.

From the mineral kingdom, to the vegetable, to animal and thence to human forms, it is mind boggling to even think how one superpower can play His vast game of chess with different lives, different species and different situations all at once. When a human being takes birth, his soul is helped to first visualise the life he will spend and in the flow of his life how he should act and interact with situations and different beings. All around him, his Guides gather and unfold a large scroll of dos and don'ts, haves and have not's, love and hate, forgiveness and bitterness etc. The Guides first try to bathe the soul in the pure waters of God's droplets of love. They try to ease out the bitterness from the soul's memories. In His kingdom of love there is no bitterness, no hatred, no evil. So a soul gets its first dose of purification before taking birth and it is made to choose first the parents whom it has interacted with in its past lives; if the option suits the soul he agrees to take birth from such a womb, otherwise if the bitterness is not washed away by the first bath, the soul can opt to be born to whomsoever it wishes to; either take revenge on its parents or otherwise – the choice is finally the soul's.

When a soul is ready to take birth, its whole life's lessons are written for him by his Guides; its destiny is chalked out, so to say. The journey starts as the seed is sown in the womb; thenceforth the soul has to finish the lessons that have been given to it; finish learning them before it can go back to its Guru. After the child grows, he loses contact with his Guides who still look after him but cannot change the course of the soul's river of life. These waters of the soul's life flow denuding and depositing his karmic dues; washing away many stones, many obstacles in the course of his life span. He emerges either purifying his being in the process or gathering dirt from his banks of life. It is therefore, up to each soul to understand and think back what he has chosen to finish. Ponder my children over God, whether you have cleansed your souls with the waters of your life or gathered mud and more dirt; this is when we say you all can change your destinies to a certain extent, when you drift away from what you have chosen to finish and interact in a different way other than His master plan.

Each soul is given a certain course to follow. A certain drama to enact and your Guides and Gurus help you to act your part as chosen. But when you try to act smarter than your directors, that is when the film of your life flops; you feel useless and you try to change positions, try to migrate like animals for greener pastures where you think life will be smoother. You all try to reach out for the rainbow of life and in doing so when you cross the rays of the harsh sun you get scorched; that is when you blame Karma.

So my children lead a simple dedicated pure life. Think not what you expect others to do for you but do what you feel is good for the betterment of your co-humanity. Each soul, if it can do one grain of good for another human soul or animal or vegetation, all combined, will make a better world, a better tomorrow and when you pass over you would have lived life as chosen. Try to erase as many mistakes from the mathematics of life. Finish your sums of life correctly and take this state of your mathematics to your Guru back with a smile on your lips and a big Thank You to Him who has given you this vast scroll of lessons to finish.

Each life thus lived will finish your karmic cycles so fast that in no time at all you will have graduated from life's college of education and will be ready to merge again into Him to help others as your Gurus have merged into eternity before you.

Live, let live, do good, don't expect returns; the interest on your investments is up above where you all ultimately belong. Lay your head on the lap of your Creator and let Him stroke your golden hair. Sleep my children. Never try to get up and leave your Creator.

Love and ooze out more love. Spread your arms like wings of a bird. Fly away and enjoy the scenic life that you have left behind. Gaze into space and into His luminous eyes.

God bless you.

The Third Eye

When a child is born in your world the soul is given a specific womb to take birth. The karmic cycle of that soul has to continue and hence, after weighing the pros and cons of past lives, the soul takes birth from a particular pair of parents. When the baby is conceived in its mother's womb, his or her third eye is still very much connected to our world so even when the child is asleep, deep in happy slumber. Happy because he still can see his Guide and Guru, in the astral world with his third eye. You might have noticed the child will either laugh or make a crying face depending on the vision he sees. The Guide protects the child and the connection between him and the Guide remains for a long, long time till such time that the child grows up in your worldly atmosphere and his memory of the astral gets sealed off for the soul to live his worldly life and finish his karmic dues which he has opted to finish.

The child grows up, goes to school, is taught by his teachers lessons which he has already learnt in his past lives but no one teaches the child to see with his third eye; a microscope of God's vast domain. But as you move towards the golden era instead of your worldly science, a child will learn to see the vastness of the cosmos like the depth of oceans and reach the astral world in the blink of his eye. His mind's eye will be so powerful that the power of thought will make him converse with his distant Guru in the astral as also his worldly relatives in the furthermost places on earth. Your telecommunication systems will be a thing of the past where mind over matter will prevail and bring all human beings together under one Guru, one Master, one language, one powerful thought. You will be able to cure ailments first by meditation or communicate with each other through projection. Your clouds of thought sent out like a bow from your third eye will be the arrow which will pierce the pores of your dear ones and interact with them.

A blind man can develop his third eye very easily and his blind instincts can lead him anywhere he wishes. In his case his Guru is always near him, protecting him, so never pity him. He is more lucky than you who have proper sight but no Guru as your cane, to follow in His footsteps. A blind man is led across to any place he wishes to be and his cane is illumined by His light which his third eye can see and follow.

So my children of God, meditate more and more each day. Try to open your third eye, which lies dormant and unexploited. Use it more. Make your real eyes blind to the light around but try to see the golden rainbows of God's horizon through the third eye. Nurture it with good thoughts, feed it with God's language of love; send out love vibes through this very third eye which will eventually lead you on to your abode in the Almighty's house of love. Sing the vibes of *Aum* and let it permeate the atmosphere; open up your third eye by exercising daily at one time, one place, one thought.

Meditation

Meditation is the song of love for God. He created man in His own image as He expected His toys to dance and sing His song of sweet melody to lull Him back to deep slumber. In His waking moments He expected His toys to spread His message of love around; to spread the fragrance of His varied rose petals for those whose sense of smell has not yet developed. Those unfortunate toys of His creation who have still to activate the springs of real life to be able to catch the notes of His song which permeates the core of His creation. These souls are still so gross they have no idea of real life and the results they have to bear in the hereafter.

Meditation is the panacea for all ailments which God never realised His handmade toys will suffer from. He made a purest of pure soul when the first handmade toy of His creation descended on earth. That human being had no desires, no jealousy, no caprice. That soul only survived to procreate God's wishes and he was in direct communication with His creator. He lived and passed over without the need for any medication. The only medication for him was nature around him. The songs of birds and the hum of bees were his sweet pills to swallow. But as years passed by he became greedy and wanted more and more of material wealth. He started drifting away from the real life and started becoming blind to God's light which he could see like a crystal ball. These souls were able to look into the future events. They could hear the sweet melody of God's music and could dance to His music of love; but at each event, each word harshly spoken, each action badly acted, man started suffering ailments of his own making; mental and physical.

As time passes, no amount of your doctor's medicine will cure you. No science will help. Man will have to revert back to medicines of yore and these are first of all purifying our mental points, your chakras which are the different springs God has placed in your physical bodies to play with. These are the strings of a guitar which God protects from harm and starts singing His song of love through this instrument, a human being.

So my children take heed. Clean your chakras. Oil your springs for God to play His music again for, very soon He will destroy these sick dilapidated toys and make new ones more sophisticated, more useful to Him; more charming with crystal clear minds for God's presence to penetrate through.

Meditation is one form of cleansing your springs of life. Sit at one time in one place. Fix your gaze inward. Don't let anyone disturb you. Concentrate and seek divine help. Let your mundane life's events pass away in front of your mind's eye like a drama. Be an actor and be a spectator. See your own life's passage of time, weigh the pros and cons of what each day has meant for you. How much of the daily bazaar have you consumed? How much is left for others who have not been able to buy their daily needs and then after weighing how much you have filled your pot of life with God's nuggets of gold...your actions...silence your mind. Let God's thoughts pass on to you with the help of your Gurus, your Guides who will act like the tunnels through which you will reach out to His light. Open your mind's eye. Let God as a doctor examine the very pores of your being. Do not let mundane material thoughts get through these tunnels of light. When you have succeeded in blanketing your vision, your mind, your hearing you will have reached a point at God's feet. Touch His lotus feet and say a big thank You to Him for having allowed you to be back in His flock again from where you all have drifted away far and wide.

So meditate daily my children of God. Let meditation be the food, the sweets, the chocolates. The purest of the pure food for your physical bodies and the proof of the pudding will be the serenity, the silent mind which you all will create again from the trash of life. That's all.

Mind Over Matter

A human mind is created by God to shine like a thousand facets of a diamond round your neck. The more you polish it the more it will glow.

When a child is born in your world, it brings along the purest diamond lodged in the human body, a computer which no one on earth can reproduce, namely your mind. As the child grows up, he or she is influenced by your so-called teachers who by teaching the wrong values of life to a child tarnish this pure diamond – the child's mind. This mind is filled with oceans of impure particles of so-called unnecessary knowledge which is transferred from a teacher's memory to his pupils. It is his ideas, his dirt, his misgivings which are pushed into a child's memory by which the innocent mind of a child is made to gather dust.

Over the years as he grows up, more and more of this filth is pushed to be stored in the mind of a child by these so-called teachers. By the end of his academic career, his mind is a storehouse of misconceptions of someone else's experiences, someone else's ideologies; by which time the facet of his brain's diamond is veiled by layers of dirt and it is too late for him to cleanse his computer virus passed on by his tutors. He grows up respecting his teachers more than his Creator. So my children of God do not let your children grow up like puppets on a string of knowledge where there is no truth, no link between his Guru, his God, his Creator.

Don't let your children drift away in the swirling waters of the filth of your world. Let his mind instead flower like a bloom in the Garden of Eden; let him be linked in meditation to his Guru. Teach him to silence his mind; give him a broom to dust away the cobwebs of wrong information stored in his computer, his mind. Let him re-polish with prayers, a damp cloth of love for Him who has put together this most sophisticated computer which no one in your world can copy. A time will come when no electronics will work – they will all be like a sick virus and only God's love and His link with humanity will survive. No one can make this mind as God has made it like a cocoon from which will emerge the most beautiful butterfly which will create more such beautiful creatures by the turn of the century.

There won't be any crime, no jealousy, no want; man will be able to produce whatever is necessary by just thinking and drawing from his bank account – his mind. So let your children learn to communicate with God. Let them devote one hour of the whole time at his disposal to say a hello to God. How else can he say a big thank you to Him who has made him.

Mind is the ultimate ladder to His abode in Heaven. Matter is only skin deep; one day you have everything, the next moment you have nothing. He controls your life like a cinema – humour God so that He plays His cinema of your life with laughter and not pathos.

Meditate and invoke God's love so that He can direct your life with laughter and not despair. God will use you as His actor and give His rewards for the best actor or actress. The final word is His so let Him be your soul, your link of love and do not chase material wants. Let the love of God be the pebbles on which to tread and walk the path where His footsteps have made a print in the sands of time. Follow Him and your life is linked eternally to Him.

That is your final goal to merge with God. Time is running out my children so concentrate on His teachings. Sing His song of love. Act His drama of life and you would have finished re-polishing your mind back to its original lustre. That's all.

Other works by the author

ABOUT THE AUTHOR

Author of eight published books and a documentary film maker, Ruzbeh N. Bharucha began his writing career in his final year of college, by editing and publishing a magazine called *Venture*. In 1992, he was appointed Associate Editor for Special Audience Publication, and two years later became the Chief Editor of the first weekly newspaper in Pune, *The Pune Tribune*, published in English and Marathi by A.K. Bhala. In 1995, he was appointed the Executive Editor, Business Publication Division, *The Indian Express*. In 2000, he edited magazines on the paranormal, mysticism, new age and travel for S.B. Associates, an editor of a monthly magazine on wellbeing. From 2008 to 2011, he was the Executive Editor of 4th D Wellbeing Journal, a widely read magazine on physical, emotional and spiritual wellness with a print run of over 60,000 copies a month. His articles have been featured in various publications, namely, *The Times of India*, *Free Press*, *The Indian Express*, *Maharashtra Herald*, *Sunday Observer*, *Jam-e-Jamshed* and *The Afternoon*.

His book, *The Fakir*, launched in October 2007 was on the top of the bestseller list in December 2007. It has been published in Hindi, Marathi and German. It is also due to be released in Punjabi, Bengali, Gujarati, Tamil and Bulgarian. It is followed by an equally successful sequel, *The Fakir: The Journey Continues...*, soon to be released in Hindi, Punjabi and German editions. *The Fakir* and *The Fakir: The Journey Continues...* have been re-printed several times and are now considered to be among the best books on spiritual and paranormal literature.

www.ruzbehbharucha.net

Join the

World Wisdom Book Club

GET THE BEST OF WORLD LITERATURE IN THE COMFORT OF YOUR HOME AT FABULOUS DISCOUNTS!

<u>Benefits of the Book Club</u>

Wherever in the world you are, you can receive the best of books at your doorstep.

- Receive FABULOUS DISCOUNTS by mail or at the **FULL CIRCLE** Bookstores in Delhi.

- Receive Exclusive Invitations to attend events being organized by **FULL CIRCLE**.

- Receive a FREE copy of the club newsletter — The World Wisdom Review — every month.

- Get UP TO 10% OFF.

Join Now!

It's simple. Just fill in the coupon overleaf and mail it to us at the address below:

FULL CIRCLE
J-40, Jorbagh Lane, New Delhi-110003
Tel: +011-24620063, 24621011 • Fax: 24645795
E-mail: contact@fullcirclebooks.in *www.fullcirclebooks.in*

Yes, I would like to be a member of the

World Wisdom Book Club

Name ☐ Mr ☐ Mrs ☐ Ms...

Mailing Address..

....

....

City....................................... Pin...

Phone.................................... Fax...

E-mail..

Profession.............................. D.O.B...................................

Areas of Interest..

....

Mail this form to:
The World Wisdom Book Club
J-40, Jorbagh Lane, New Delhi-110003
Tel: +011-24620063, 24621011 • Fax: 24645795
E-mail: contact@fullcirclebooks.in *www.fullcirclebooks.in*

THE LAST MARATHON